Rudy Allison
June, 15, 1986

**Hidden Corners
Of
New
England**

Hidden Corners of New England

Written and Illustrated by

David Yeadon

Funk & Wagnalls
New York

Copyright © 1976 by David Yeadon

All rights reserved. Except for use in a review, the reproduction or utilization of this work in any form or by any electronic, mechanical, or other means, now known or hereafter invented, including xerography, photocopying, and recording, and in any information storage and retrieval system is forbidden without the written permission of the publisher. Published simultaneously in Canada by Fitzhenry & Whiteside Limited, Toronto.

Designed by David Yeadon & Judith Woracek

Manufactured in the United States of America

Library of Congress Cataloging in Publication Data

Yeadon, David.
   Hidden corners of New England.

   Includes index.
   1. New England—Description and travel—1951–
—Guide-books. I. Title.
F2.3.Y42   917.4'04'4   75-42072
ISBN 0-308-10240-1
ISBN 0-308-10241-X (pbk.)
10 9 8 7 6 5 4 3 2 1

For Doug and Willie

Books Written and Illustrated by David Yeadon

Exploring Small Towns: Vol. I—Southern California

Exploring Small Towns: Vol. II—Northern California

Hidden Restaurants of Southern California

Hidden Restaurants of Northern California

Sumptuous Indulgence on a Shoestring—a cookbook

Wine Tasting in California

The New York Book of Bars, Pubs and Taverns

. . . from all around-
Earth and her waters, and the depths of air-
Comes a still voice:-

From "Thanatopsis"—William Cullen Bryant

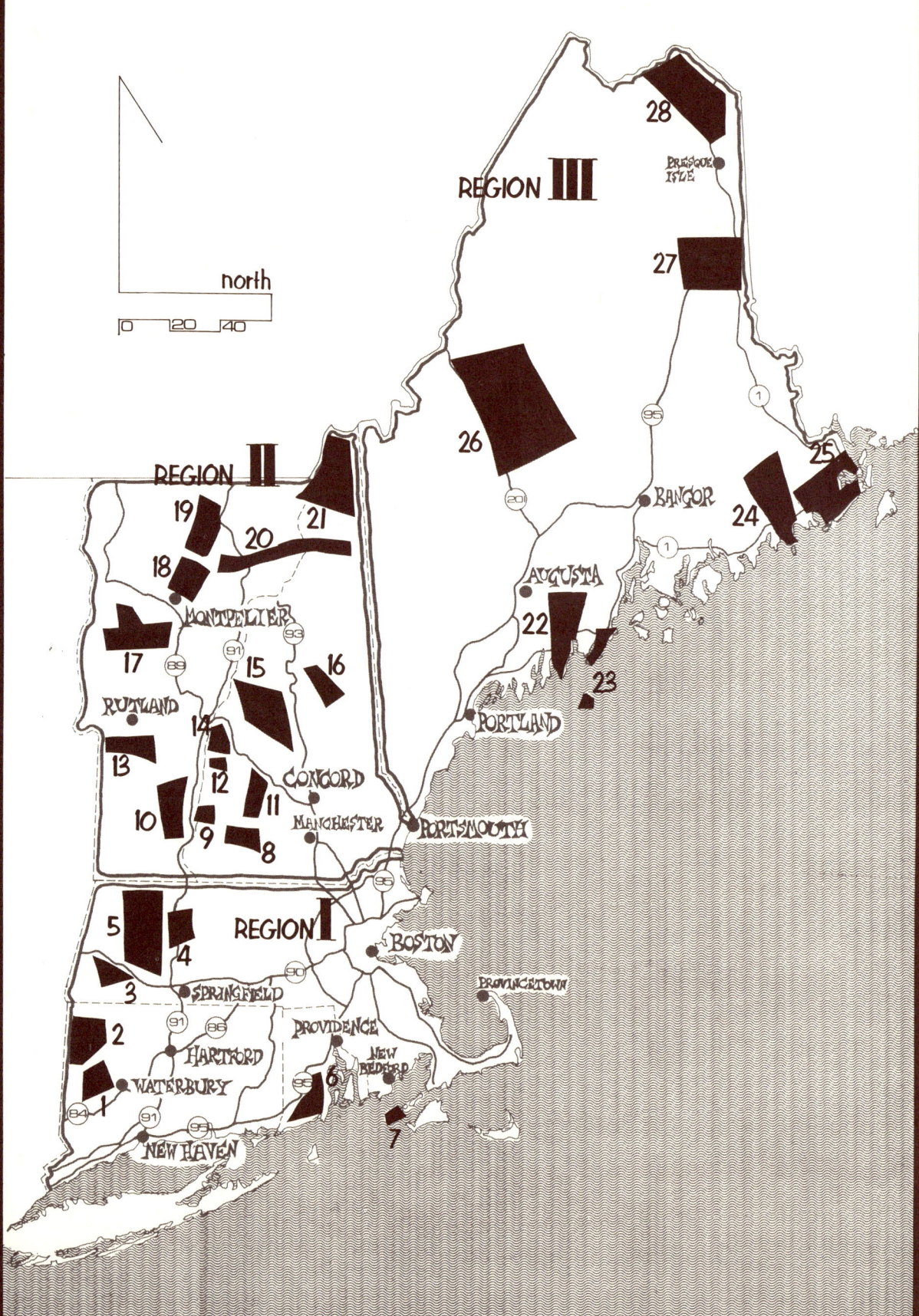

Contents

EXPLORING HIDDEN CORNERS　　　　　　　　　　　　　　　　　　　　　*1*

Region I: Connecticut, Massachusetts and Rhode Island

1. WOODBURY AND VICINITY   Home of the Yankee Spirit　　　　　8
2. CORNWALL AND VICINITY   Strange Tales of the Forest　　　　14
3. THE DALE OF TYRINGHAM   A Hidden Home for the Shakers　　20
4. HATFIELD AND VICINITY   A Segment of Pioneer Valley　　　　24
5. THE NORTHERN BERKSHIRES   The "Still Voice" of the Mountains　　30
6. THE GREAT RHODE ISLAND SWAMP   Massacre of the Narragansetts　　36
7. CUTTYHUNK ISLAND   A Place to Enjoy Your Own Company　　40

Region II: Vermont and New Hampshire

8. MONADNOCK AND THE SOUTHERN LAKES   A Kingdom of the Muse　　48
9. BELLOWS FALLS   An Interesting Example of Townscape　　54
10. CHESTER AND VICINITY   The Curious Legend of Clarence Adams　　58
11. THE SUTTONS TO WASHINGTON   A Brief but Beautiful Drive　　64
12. CLAREMONT   Elaborate Urbanity in a Pastoral Setting　　70
13. CLARENDON SPRINGS AND VICINITY   Springs and Spas of the Green Mountains　　74
14. CORNISH AND VICINITY   Artists, Writers and "Lincoln-Shaped Men"　　80
15. CANAAN AND THE NORTHERN LAKES   Lakes, Ponds and Pools　　85
16. SANDWICH AND VICINITY   Moses Hall and the Sandwich Notch　　91
17. BRISTOL AND THE LINCOLN GAP   Fall in the Green Mountains　　95
18. THE MONTPELIER LAKE COUNTRY   Some Notable Vermont Characters　　102
19. THE CRAFTSBURYS   A Tangle of Back Roads　　108
20. MILAN TO GREENSBORO BEND   A Long Mountain Drive　　114
21. PITTSBURG AND VICINITY   New England's Frontier Republic　　122

Region III: Maine

22.	THE BRISTOL PENINSULA Pemaquid, Pirates and Lobster Pots	130
23.	MONHEGAN Journey to a Small Island	136
24.	JONESPORT AND VICINITY The Unusual Voyage of Pastor Adams	143
25.	EASTPORT/LUBEC A Quiet Stretch of Coast, Rich in History	149
26.	THE GUILFORD/JACKMAN LOOP On the Edge of the Allagash	156
27.	HOULTON AND VICINITY Where the Potato Is King	163
28.	THE ST. JOHN VALLEY The Acadian Land of Evangeline	169
	INDEX	177

Exploring Hidden Corners

I remember the evening I completed this book. I was sitting at a table strewn with paper, pens, photographs, sketches, newspaper articles, recording tapes—all the paraphernalia of writing. In front of me was a small window that looked out over some bushes at the harbor below. Fishing boats, clustered around the wharves, sat motionless in the water. It was autumn and the sun was already low, a big bronze ball suspended just above the pointed tips of the conifers on the far side of the inlet.

I left the table and walked outside into the cool air. There was no sound; no birds called, no crickets chirped. Even the gentle slapping and lapping of the water against the boats had ceased. It was that time of evening when everything seems to pause for a while before dusk, before night.

I strolled down the hill from the cottage and along one of the wharves. The planks creaked. I sat at the end by a pile of lobster pots and dangled my feet over the edge. Then, slowly, in the stillness, I thought of all the places I had seen during my travels in New England—those little enclaves away from the bustling highways, where the pace of life is gentle and change comes very, very slowly. I thought of all the people I had met: families whose hospitality I enjoyed, farmers who described the land and its mysteries, children who told me eerie folktales of the mountains and forests and frightened themselves in the process, other travelers like myself who love the quiet places and the back roads.

I thought of crisp mornings when frost-flecked fields gleamed like beaten silver in the sharp, bright sun. I recalled the tiny white villages wrapped in autumn mists, the smell of freshly caught fish cooking in hot butter, the sudden sweeping vistas of mountains from tracks high in the hills, the sound of villagers singing together in church on a Sunday morning, the deep shadows of summer on a white clapboard house. I remembered finding waterfalls in the heart of silent woods, the smell of hay in an old gray barn, eating apples picked fresh from a roadside tree, watching a thunderstorm swirl across the mountains.

When I looked at the harbor again, it was almost dark. The sun had disappeared, leaving a dull red streak along the horizon. A breeze blew in off the sea and the water began its familiar lapping against the boats and wharves. I walked back up the hill to the cottage and put away my pens and papers.

The book was finished.

I had set out to sketch and write about those hidden corners of New England rarely visited by most tourists. Not that I have anything against tourists or places to which they are attracted; it's just that I prefer the rough, unpaved back roads to the major highways, the little-known villages to the more legendary historic centers, a small country inn to an elaborate motel. Fortunately I seem to be part of a minority, and I like it that way. The only reason I wrote the book was to share my experiences and interests with others of like mind, who prefer to explore those areas that express the true character and diversity of New England.

This is not a how-to-get-there-and-what-to-do book. I have not provided extensive travel directions, detailed maps, hotel and restaurant recommendations or stop-and-look suggestions. Occasionally I have offered warnings where road conditions are likely to be bad or where the chance of getting completely lost in a signless territory is high. But generally the book is for travelers like myself, who enjoy the thrills and surprises of exploring little-known parts of the countryside with only the sun and common sense as guides. Of course such guides are not infallible—but fortunately I also enjoy getting lost. In fact some of the most memorable experiences during my explorations of New England occurred when I abandoned maps and followed random lanes at will, sketching hidden villages, sitting by quiet lakes, dozing in cozy hollows.

For those who decide to follow me on these meandering journeys, I offer the following words of advice.

Maps: In general, the maps of southern and northern New England distributed by gasoline companies are adequate for locating most of the places mentioned in this book (I found the Mobil versions particularly useful). More detailed maps of the individual states, usually available at tourist information centers, are better for back road travel, but these are occasionally inaccurate and in most cases show only a limited selection of the available unpaved roads. So reconcile yourself to the likelihood that you will often become lost—and enjoy the experience!

Road Signs: Although directional signs, mileage indicators and community markers are abundant in the more popular sections of New England, they disappear almost entirely in the lesser-known, hidden corners. There seems to be an assumption that the only people traveling in these areas are residents and thus signs are superfluous. So the hidden-corner explorer must rely on his maps, common sense and a willingness to stop and ask directions. Occasionally this last practice may elicit ambiguous Yankee comments, but in most cases I found people to be friendly, helpful and even generously hospitable. Some of my best meals in New England were enjoyed in the homes of back country families who took pity on a poor, lost traveler.

Accommodations: There is inevitably a lack of accommodations outside the more popular tourist areas. Fortunately though in New England distances are short, and even in the most obscure regions travelers are normally within reasonable driving distance of hotels, inns and restaurants. Obviously, during the peak summer and fall months some advance reservations may be necessary; if this is not possible the traveler should seriously consider carrying camping equipment. Campsites are well distributed throughout the six states and, with the exception of some of the more popular state park sites, space is usually available most months of the year.

Historical Sites and Other Tourist Attractions: This book is not intended as a guide to tourist-oriented facilities, and well-publicized historical sites, "preserved" villages, museums and other popular attractions are only occasionally mentioned. These are normally indicated on most travel maps of New England, and guidebooks and pamphlets that describe such facilities are available in abundance at book stores and tourist information offices.

I have divided the six-state area of New England into three distinctive regions:

Region I: Connecticut, Massachusetts and Rhode Island.
Region II: Vermont and New Hampshire.
Region III: Maine.

The hidden corners were chosen to reflect each region's character, scenery and history, including its legends and folktales, its heroes and, occasionally, its catastrophes. In all honesty, however, I should add that they were chosen mainly because I enjoyed being there. Each corner has its own particular beauty and appeal, yet together they provide a glimpse of New England both as it once was and as it is today. While I cannot claim to have revealed every facet of this incredibly beautiful "Diamond of Our Nation," I trust you, the reader and traveler, will be fascinated by these diverse explorations as much as I was.

May you enjoy all your journeys.

**Region I:
Connecticut,
Massachusetts
and
Rhode Island**

King Solomon's Temple—Woodbury

1. WOODBURY AND VICINITY
Home of the Yankee Spirit

The terms "New Englander" and "Yankee" were once considered to be virtually synonymous. However, when first used, "Yankee" applied more often to the spirit of the individual than to his place of origin. It referred to that special intransigence of purpose which often characterized the more notable inhabitants and folk heroes of New England. In this regard, there are few regions that match the Yankee flavor of the towns nestled between the Shepaug and Pomperaug Rivers in western Connecticut—Woodbury, Roxbury, Washington and South Britain.

Woodbury is an attractive roadside community built on a flat ledge of land above the Pomperaug River and below the steep hills that frame the eastern side of the valley. Large homes in a range of New England and mid-Victorian styles line the long, tree-shaded main street and give the town a prosperous, if slightly conservative, character, similar to that found in such other distinguished Connecticut communities as Newtown, Sharon, and Litchfield. By way of an architectural climax, the southern entrance to the town is dominated by the Masonic headquarters, King Solomon's Temple, set atop a sheer rockface.

Woodbury's early growth was characterized by the rebelliousness of its founders, religious dissidents from the Stratford community, who founded the Second Church of Stratford and moved out into the wilderness to create their own plantation in 1672. Division and usage of property was defined in detail according to the community's Fundamental Articles, and the settlers went to great pains to ensure legal land purchase from the Indians, although confusion between local tribes over ownership often meant that certain sectors of land were actually acquired as many as three separate times during the late 1600s!

Following a brief migration back to Stratford in 1675 to avoid conflict with the Indians during King Philip's War, the community settled down to steady growth until around the time of the Revolution, when the Yankee spirit emerged in full bloom. Woodbury and the Pomperaug Valley became a center for followers of Ethan Allen, who, some historians claim, was born in nearby Roxbury instead of the more commonly accepted birthplace of Litchfield, farther to the north. Anti-Tory sentiment ran high. Woodbury's Episcopalian rector, John Marshall, was a staunch Tory and had no qualms about his beliefs. On every occasion he could manage, including the Sunday sermon, he courageously gave vent to his opinions. According to a local historian, William Cothren, he narrowly escaped bodily harm a number of times by hiding in a secret chamber

Washington

Seth Warner Memorial—Roxbury

behind the chimney of his rectory. After one particularly critical tirade from the pulpit, he was obliged to remain there for a whole week until the following Sunday, when he emerged again to rant at the villagers. Although a Tory by intellectual persuasion, Reverend Marshall possessed many of the traits of a true Yankee.

A few miles to the west, over some of the steepest terrain in the state, is the community of Washington. Whichever way you approach the village, you're in for a long, winding climb up through dark woods until you reach the town green. But it's all worth it, for here is one of the most attractive rural scenes in southern New England. In the center of the green, surrounded by fine old trees, is the richly detailed church, boasting a deep portico with double column supports. Unlike many of the churches in the region that often seem to have been assembled in odd bits and pieces over a number of decades, the Washington church has an essential dignity and harmony that come from unified architectural expression. In fact, the whole village seems to possess a distinct visual unity. Most of the old wooden homes surrounding the green are painted pristine white with dark olive detailing, and, in contrast to other communities in the region, their style is classically restrained. There are no elaborate Victorian/Gothic extravagances here and the buildings are almost secondary to the green itself, which undulates under the trees and laps against the wicker fences and doorsteps. It's always quiet in Washington, although spring is the best time to visit—especially for a long, restful weekend at the Mayflower Inn, a beautiful old establishment set in wooded grounds nearby.

Ironically, this peaceful hilltop village was the scene of such severe Tory/Patriot conflict during the Revolution that even families were split by the dissension. The Stone brothers, Joel and Lehman, lived together in a house (the "Red House") near the green, until Lehman's pro-British sympathies led to their separation in 1774. After it was announced that Lehman had joined the British army, the house was divided exactly down the middle and his portion was confiscated by the community. Similar actions were taken against other local Tories, and by 1779 Washington had become such an anti-Tory enclave that it separated from the town of Woodbury, of which it was part, in protest over the "tolerance" of Woodbury residents.

One of the most famous Patriot characters in the area was Ethan Allen's sturdy companion Seth Warner, whose name is associated with many of the rebellious exploits of the Green Mountain Boys. He was born at Roxbury in May 1743 and, although he spent much of his life around Bennington in Vermont, was buried in Roxbury Green beneath a large memorial that praises the "bravery, sagacity, energy and humanity" of this Yankee giant.

Washington's main contribution to the Yankee spirit of the region was Frederick W. Gunn, who was born in the village in 1816 and later founded his famous school, the Gunnery, here, on the simple premise that social, physical and moral development is as important as intellectual skill. Gunn was a remarkable man who often wore the kilt, cap and sporran of his ancestral family, the Scottish McLean clan. He spoke his mind with no hesitation or fear. Of the Bible he once wrote, "I believe it to be inspired, but not to be infallible"; and he was among the first in the area to vehemently oppose "the abominable system of slavery," following a visit to the South, which he described as "worse than I ever thought it could be."

The Gunn Library and the adjoining Museum, located just off the green, remain as memorials to this upright and outspoken man. It says much for his influence that the school he founded over one hundred years ago still thrives today in a series of tastefully designed buildings on the southern fringe of the village. (Subsequently the well-known girl's school Wykeham Rise was founded in an equally attractive setting a mile or so to the north of Washington.) Another local individualist, William Hamilton Gibson, is also commemorated in the Gunn Museum. His superbly illustrated books *Pastoral Days* and *Strolls by Starlight and Sunshine* reflect his great love and understanding of nature, much of it gleaned from walks and study in the Washington area.

It was men such as these—artists, educators, soldiers, and even the occasional priest—who translated the early colonists' desire for independent control over their own affairs into an exciting reality. They were

South Britain

stubborn, persevering men, but more than that they also possessed the Yankee talent for ingenuity in the face of adversity. The day of the Yankee peddler, with his indispensable supply of notions and potions, soon yielded to the emergence of the Yankee entrepreneur, characterized by his canny ability to adapt, improvise, invent, and ingeniously turn any occurrence to his own advantage. This trait was particularly valuable after the War for Independence, when the termination of links with Britain meant the colonists had to fend entirely for themselves. And what a challenge that provided, what frantic activity fired these tiny communities: iron ore smelting, granite polishing, cutlery manufacturing, an "epidemic of hat shops" at Roxbury and Southbury, knitting of cashmere shawls (sent to First Avenue in Manhattan for special printing), cider mills, silversmithing, factories that turned out satinette, cigars, pottery, furniture—even the manufacture of buttons and suspenders and the production of carpets in the tiny, straggling community of South Britain, whose only notable feature today is its stately church, just across from the local general store.

As with other parts of New England that experienced a similar surge of industrialization following independence, little remains now. Companies grew, merged and centralized closer to the ports and other transportation facilities. Mass production soon eradicated most of the small village factories, and the area regained its pastoral character. Today Washington, Roxbury and South Britain provide a picture of New England life as it must have been before the Revolution.

In a similar, although more unusual, way, the tiny community of Churaevka, near Lakeside on the Housatonic River, provides a picture of Russian life as it must have been prior to that country's revolution. It was founded in 1920 by Count Ilya Tolstoi, grandson of the famous writer, as a quiet retreat for displaced White Russians. Its simply constructed homes set on large, open lawns suggest the *dachas,* or summer homes, commonly found in the mountains of Russia. The tiny Ukrainian-style church, almost invisible from the main road, provides the final touch of authenticity.

Churaevka is by no means a tourist attraction, as there's very little to see beyond the lines of mailboxes painted with such names as Romanoff, Shoonsky, Osypczuk and Alexandrow. Many of the homes are hidden down private roads, and the community itself is most difficult to find. Yet somehow its location is appropriate, for in the seventeenth century, only a few miles to the north, similar groups of "foreigners" began to build their own communities in the rolling hills around Woodbury.

Church—Churaevka

2. CORNWALL AND VICINITY
Strange Tales of the Forest

Its proximity to the increasingly popular village of Litchfield has led to the recent discovery of sections of the Cornwall region, and a gradual influx of commercialism. However, this remains one of the most beautiful areas in western Connecticut, and most of it is likely to remain unspoiled for a long time to come. Explorers should avoid the main highways and travel the rambling roads and tracks that traverse the steep hills and quiet valleys around Goshen, Milton, Cornwall and Sharon. Losing oneself is all part of the fun; don't look for road signs because they are few and far between. Instead, follow the dusty tracks through the thick forests covering most of the area, past old farms and barns, and find your own hidden corners.

The best place to start is West Cornwall, a small hillside community overlooking the Housatonic River. Its main street contains a dozen or so buildings, a few with fine Victorian detailing, framing the old covered bridge across the river. Although recently the village has become a little more tourist-oriented, due partially to the popularity of the nearby Housatonic Meadows campsite, it still has an unspoiled character. Martin Gold's book and bric-a-brac store, in a gray Victorian villa at the top end of the street above the now disused railroad tracks, is the kind of place you can browse for hours. Downstairs is the old bottles, jewelry and mis-

Farm scene—near Cornwall

cellaneous antiques department. Upstairs, in the former bedrooms, are row upon row of musty books set among unopened packing crates, and cardboard cartons filled with more books or ancient back issues of *Life* and *National Geographic*. For all the apparent chaos here there's a distinct order, known only to Martin. Whatever the subject, he will lead you unwaveringly to the exact shelf and, if given a precise enough description, to the actual book you require.

A few miles to the southeast along narrow, winding roads through the forest is the sleepy town of Cornwall, located just far enough from the main route to preserve its unchanged character. The old lantern and spring bell by the entrance to the local community hall are still used as they were almost a hundred years ago. Little has changed. There are no discordant elements of commercialism here. The fine porticoed church watches over the green where the Foreign Mission School was founded in 1817 as a center for the education of Hawaiian and Indian missionaries. In the local cemetery is the grave of Henry Obookiah, a converted heathen priest from the Sandwich Islands, who died here while still a student at the school. Unfortunately this experiment in international relations ended rather abruptly in 1826, when local indignation reached fever pitch following the marriage of two Cornwall maidens to Indian students.

For all their bigotry, the citizens of Cornwall remained proud of a onetime resident of somewhat dubious character, Colonel Mathew Lyon. He was exactly the kind of endearing rogue that New England historians love to produce as evidence of the region's vigorous and vital population. Here's one description of "Spitting Mat," or, as he later became known, the "Dragon of Democracy," taken from an early-twentieth-century work: "Mathew Lyon was a romantic and conspicuous figure of his day—an Irish run-away, redemptioner, soldier, publisher, printer, editor, author, lumberman, miller, inventor; prosperous and bankrupt; cashiered and promoted; convicted and elected to Congress while still in jail; married first to a niece of General Ethan Allen and next to the daughter of one Governor, and later to the daughter-in-law of another. . . ."

Mat first gained fame as one of the rebels who, with Ethan Allen, captured Fort Ticonderoga from the British on May 10, 1775. Later he helped move the great Ticonderoga cannons to Boston, where they were used by George Washington to force the Redcoats out of the city. As a reward for valiant service he was made paymaster of the Vermont militia, and in 1782 colonel of a regiment of the Green Mountain Boys. He also began publication of a powerful bimonthly magazine, *The Scourge of the Aristocracy,* and later, following a period in the Vermont legislature, was elected to Congress, where he gained a notorious reputation after forcing a fellow representative into a duel on the floor of the House—fire tongs versus walking cane! Not long afterward Lyon found himself in jail under the Sedition Act for criticizing President John Adams, but at his trial he presented such a well-argued and passionate defense that he was re-elected to Congress in 1799 and was carried to the Capitol in triumph at the head of a twelve-mile line of supporters. A truly unusual and remarkable man!

Main Street—West Cornwall

A little to the south of the main street in Cornwall, reached by an unmarked track, is one of the most beautiful stretches of ancient forest in Connecticut, the Cathedral Pines. Within the soft shade of this virgin stand of white pine are no sounds other than the whisper of high branches and an occasional bird call. Few people come here, and the place retains its utter peace. The same can be said of another section of woodland nearby, although the reasons for the silence here are mysterious and chilling. This is the "Dark Entry"—a gloomy tangle of stunted vegetation, home of the great horned owl, a place filled with rustlings and the moan of wind through the dead trees. It is by no means an attractive area, and local folktales of unmarked graves deep in its recesses and of hunters driven mad by sights they could never describe do not encourage casual exploration.

The whole region around the Cornwalls, a terrain of deep hills and dense woods, has many contrasting moods. On a bright summer day, when sunlight filters through a filigree of branches and leaves, and soft shadows prance on rocks and across the sparkling surface of streams, the spirit is gay—almost effervescent. But walk the same paths on a dark day, or when the damp fogs settle on the mountains, and one will find the somberness of the gray gloom all too conducive to belief in the eerie tales told of these woods and their mysterious inhabitants.

There were once many tiny communities hereabout—hidden-away places with such strange names as Hogback, Wildcat, Mast Swamp, Indian Lane and Dudley Town. The last of these was home to early English charcoal makers, and was for a while a prosperous little place, until epidemics, attacks of mental illness and eventually a series of gruesome murders led to its rapid demise in the early eighteenth century.

Residents of Milton, a little town to the southeast of Cornwall, have a healthy respect for the folklore of the area. One old gentleman, who had lived in the nearby hills most of his life, told me that "strangers should be careful in these parts. These woods have a way all of their own." He was reluctant to elaborate—and I was reluctant to press him—but eventually he added, "The worst fear in these woods, you know, is the fear from inside yourself." We left it at that.

Opposite the church that faces across the wide expanse of village green in Milton is a hollow where the town pond was once located. Here in the mid-1800s a series of engineering experiments were conducted by John Griswold on a scaled-down vessel similar in concept to John Ericsson's famous *Monitor,* which routed the Confederacy's ironclad battleship *Merrimac (Virginia)* in 1862. Although their ideas seem almost identical the two never met, and nothing more was heard of Mr. Griswold's boat following its brief career on the pond.

Milton in the nineteenth century was once highly praised by Henry Ward Beecher, who lived nearby in Litchfield, for "the commanding performance of its pulpit." Apparently at that time its religious prowess was matched by its considerable industrial activity, which included five sawmills, two gristmills, an ironworks, one trip hammer, one wool-carding

Milton

machine, one machine for manufacturing wooden clocks and two shoe makers, as well as six schoolhouses. Today, however, Milton is a sleepy remnant of its former glory. All that remains is a rather lonely church and a few pleasant cottages set against a backdrop of dark forest.

Of course, most of the industry has gone from the region as a whole. Over in the west the settlements of Kent and Sharon, linked by a superb mountain road through Macedonia State Park, were both famous for their iron ore, blast furnaces and foundries. Farther to the north near Salisbury the ore was of such pure quality that the area experienced a frantic iron rush in 1732 and grew at an amazing rate, until the development of mines in the American West led to its decline after 1800.

Sharon today is an exclusive hilltop community, similar both in character and in the wealth of its residents to Litchfield. It was at a forge a few miles from town that the redoubtable Ethan Allen cast cannon for the Continental Army and gathered about him a band of local followers whom he described as "as good a regiment of marksmen and scalpers as America can afford."

The forges at Sharon turned out a remarkable variety of products during the heyday of the iron industry in the area. However, its economic base was always more diversified than that of adjoining communities, and at one time the villagers produced not only cigars, shoes and mousetraps but also raised silkworms on the white mulberry trees that still line Main

Street today. Many citizens became so wealthy that they were able to import stonemasons from Italy to construct their great mansions. The clocktower, constructed in 1885, at the lower end of Main Street is a fine example of their work, although the setting of this red and gray granite monolith against the gently rolling hills of the Housatonic Valley seems a little incongruous. Also, readers who visit the spot will note that in my sketch I have indulged in artistic license and omitted the urban tangle of road signs and telephone wires that wreck the visual harmony of this part of the town. Fortunately, however, the remainder of the community is well preserved and contains a few fine specimens of eighteenth-century residential architecture.

Somehow, though, even when walking the elegant streets of Sharon, I find it hard to forget those strange folktales of the forest—the forest that seems to envelop so closely this hidden corner of Connecticut.

Clock tower—Sharon

Farm scene—near Tyringham

3. THE DALE OF TYRINGHAM
A Hidden Home for the Shakers

The night's rain had left translucent strips of clouds in the hills. They wafted like long banners, and the rough road steamed as the first bright shafts of morning sun warmed its surface. It was strangely quiet. I had heard the dawn chorus earlier, every moist warble and chirp, but now there was little sound other than the rustling of leaves as drops of dew dripped downward from the higher branches of the trees that formed a natural canopy over the road, framing the view northward. The view had made me pause.

Below—far below—was a long, narrow valley, enclosed on both sides by steep hills. The fields, different shades of green and beige, were crisply defined by fences and hedgerows. A white spire rose from a cluster of trees. Large barns, a few newly painted red but most grayed by the elements, sat alone in the fields or close to narrow cart tracks. A stream meandered the length of the valley, trailed by trees. Nothing moved. There was no sound from the valley.

It must have been this peaceful prospect that first attracted the Shakers in 1792. Prior to that time a few settlers had collected here and learned the art of maple sugar making from the local Indians, but the Massachusetts agrarian economy had slumped after the Revolution. Even Shays' uprising in 1786 (see "Hatfield and Vicinity"—page 24) made little difference to the disgruntled farmers, and Tyringham, along with many other parts of the state, remained unchanged for decades.

That was just fine for the Shakers, or, as they later called themselves, the United Society of Believers. One of their prime aims was to pursue their crafts and beliefs in total seclusion. They had suffered quite enough—particularly back home in Manchester, England, where the movement had begun in 1747, as a development of the then popular socialistically oriented religious sects. In 1774 a small group under Ann Lee, their leader, came to America, but some of their early experiences in New England were equally unpleasant. It was only after their ever increasing numbers had founded a series of secluded settlements that the attentions of the populace were diverted to other, even more unusual revival groups such as the Merry Dancers, the New Lights and the Comeouters.

The Tyringham Valley was one such isolated location. However, rather than build on the valley floor, the Shakers founded their community of Fernside on the wooded slopes of Mount Horeb, following a grade that gave them homes of two stories on the upper side and four stories on the lower. Here, halfway between their neat valley farms and their mystical tabernacle on the summit of the mountain, they lived in relative tranquility for almost a hundred years.

The Shakers were particularly well known for the quality and practicality of their products, most notably their furniture and their wooden hand rakes. In 1884 one of Tyringham's three shops turned out 48,000 such implements. However, by that time the community had largely disintegrated as the Shaker "adventure" dwindled significantly. Many members had gone "to the world." In the single year 1858, twenty-three of the one hundred believers at Tyringham departed. Today nothing remains of Fernside except a few scattered overgrown cellar holes.

The demise of the Shaker movement was hardly noticed in the industrial furor that swept Massachusetts and the other New England states in the early and middle 1800s. The British and French blockades during the War of 1812 had reduced America's effectiveness as a trading nation and encouraged, instead, the development of a self-sufficient economy. In addition, the New England farmers suffered from the opening of the Erie Canal in 1825, which allowed the less expensive Ohio grain and produce to be marketed in the coastal states.

Many moved west, but the most indomitable Yankees remained to establish an industrial base in the region. Soon there was hardly a village without its own mill, cannery, distillery or—as in the case of the Tyringham area—paper factory. Such nearby towns as Lee, Lenox, Mill River, New Marlboro and Southfield also possessed their own paper plants, some of which still operate today, but the mill in Tyringham was the piece de resistance of the area. It began with hand-operated machines that produced one sheet at a time. The later introduction of the refined cylinder process in no way affected quality, and at the New York

Crystal Palace World's Fair of 1853, Tyringham Bond was chosen by international judges as the finest writing paper in the world.

As I travel the tranquil New England villages of today I often find it hard to imagine the vigor, the energy, the pounding of machines, the rush of waterwheels, the clatter of carts on their way to market—the dynamic pace at which these little communities used to operate. Tyringham in particular is so sleepy on a summer's day that the dogs even ignore the cats, and the stillness of the valley wraps the old homes and the white church on the hill in a silent cocoon. The only place with occasional life is the library, where Mark Twain, who summered here in 1903, left a signed collection of his work. Otherwise the village slumbers alongside its brook, from which all remnants of the old paper mill have been removed.

Farther down the road, toward Lee, is an unusual structure that local enthusiasts intend to maintain in perpetuity as an art gallery and a memorial to its designer and creator, Sir Henry Kitson. This unique gentleman, best known for his "Minute Man" sculpture at Lexington, was born in 1865 only a few miles east of Shaker leader Ann Lee's home in Manchester, England—although had they met, the two would have found little in common. Kitson's was one of the most respected literary and artistic

Kitson Mansion—Tyringham

families in Huddersfield, a Yorkshire woolen-mill town, whereas the Lees were merely part of Manchester's vast underprivileged working class.

Kitson left England in 1877 to join his brother's stonecarving establishment in New York, and he was soon involved in elaborate commissions for the Astors and Vanderbilts. A brief period at L'Ecole des Beaux-Arts in Paris was followed by his triumph at the 1889 Paris Exposition, where he was the only sculptor from America to receive an award medal. His fame as a creator of memorials, particularly commemorating notable events of American history, led to the "Minute Man" commission in 1897 and, inevitably, to a great accumulation of wealth.

And what better way for an artist to use his wealth than in the creation of an "ultimate studio"? So, during the 1930s, Sir Henry designed and supervised the construction of his Santarella estate by a group of English carpenters imported for the task, in a quiet corner of the Tyringham dale. Two existing silos were converted into Gothic-spired structures, and the main studio supports a Gaudi-like roof of bronze and brown shingles, inspired by the autumnal rolling hills of the Berkshires. Without doubt Sir Henry's structure is one of the most outstanding examples of individualized architecture in New England, and a suitable memorial to the spirit of the valley where many unusual souls have found peace and joy.

Town hall—Whately

4. HATFIELD AND VICINITY
A Segment of Pioneer Valley

I first saw Tobacco Valley from the town hall lawn in Whately, on one of those pristine New England mornings. The town hall itself is perched on the edge of a steep ridge that drops abruptly to the neat green fields far below. Away in the distance were the University of Massachusetts towers at Amherst; directly across, the scarlet peak of Mount Sugarloaf rose out of the valley floor, and the Connecticut River—wide and rather brown following two days of summer thunderstorms—meandered sluggishly southward through the fields. The only discordant element was a number of large square patches of white, scattered irregularly throughout the valley and its foothills. These, I learned later, were the tobacco fields, acres upon acres of fertile earth covered entirely by loosely woven cotton sheets. They are not so abundant as they once were—onions, corn and potatoes are now the dominant valley crops—but they are sufficient to create a most unusual sight when viewed from the surrounding hills.

It's difficult to appreciate the turbulent history of this pastoral region, appropriately named Pioneer Valley. Not only were its early settlements regularly gutted by the Indians and the French, and their populations massacred or marched as captives into Canada, but the area also was a hotbed of discontent during Shays' Rebellion in the 1780s. It was in Hatfield, a charming town of fine Victorian homes set along a wide, tree-lined street, that representatives of fifty western Massachusetts communities gathered at the meetinghouse in 1786 to formulate their "Twenty-five Grievances" against the quality of American government following the War of Independence. Later in that year Daniel Shays found himself, at first reluctantly, the leader of a thousand rebellious farmers who marched on the courts at Springfield to emphasize their frustration. At the national level financial affairs were in total disarray. Most of the wartime troops had not been paid, foreign trade was negligible due to Britain's closure of its own ports and those of the Empire to American goods and, to top it all, there was no soundly established currency. At the local level great discontent was voiced over the inflated salaries being awarded to petty government officials (inevitably leading to inflated taxes) and the aristocratic background and attitudes of state senators particularly. Many citizens doubted the benefits of the Revolution and decided to use the same machinery of rebellion that had ousted the British to correct their new government.

It all began rather slowly in towns like Hatfield, with lists of grievances and "Committees of Correspondence." Then, as momentum developed, Shays became an effective leader, and for a while during the late 1780s it looked as if the country was on the verge of a major internal war. In fact it was only through the use of a large federal force of five thousand soldiers under General Benjamin Lincoln that peace was eventually restored, after a confrontation with the rebels at the Springfield arsenal and a pursuit through snowbound Massachusetts that lasted ten days.

Following the rout the government intended to hang all captured rebels. However, public opinion was such that most were eventually pardoned—including Daniel Shays, who retired to Sparta, New York, for the remainder of his life, and was even awarded a government pension!

The rather gentlemanly conduct of many of these skirmishes and confrontations, in which lives were only rarely lost, contrasts harshly with the experiences of early pioneers in the valley. At first relations with the local Pocumtuc Indians were congenial. Land was purchased through agreement. Hatfield, for example, cost the original settlers "three hundred fathoms of wampum and sundry gifts." But peace was short-lived as a small plaque in the town's main street shows; in 1677 Isaac and John Graves, sons of an English settler, were murdered by members of a valley tribe. Only two years previously the villagers had fought off a concerted attack by eight hundred Indians during which many homes were burned. This was a time of fierce conflict with New England Indians led by Metacom, or, as he was better known, "King Philip" (see "The Great Rhode Island Swamp"—page 36). It is said that a large rock jutting out of the face of nearby Mount Sugarloaf provided a control point for Philip during the battle. From there he watched his warriors retreat from Hatfield, followed by many of the local settlers and troops. As cleverly prearranged, the Indians waited while their pursuers walked straight into ambush in the dense valley scrub. Eventually the whites were forced to make a hasty and disorganized retreat, leaving behind several scouts who died long and gruesome deaths at the hands of the Indians.

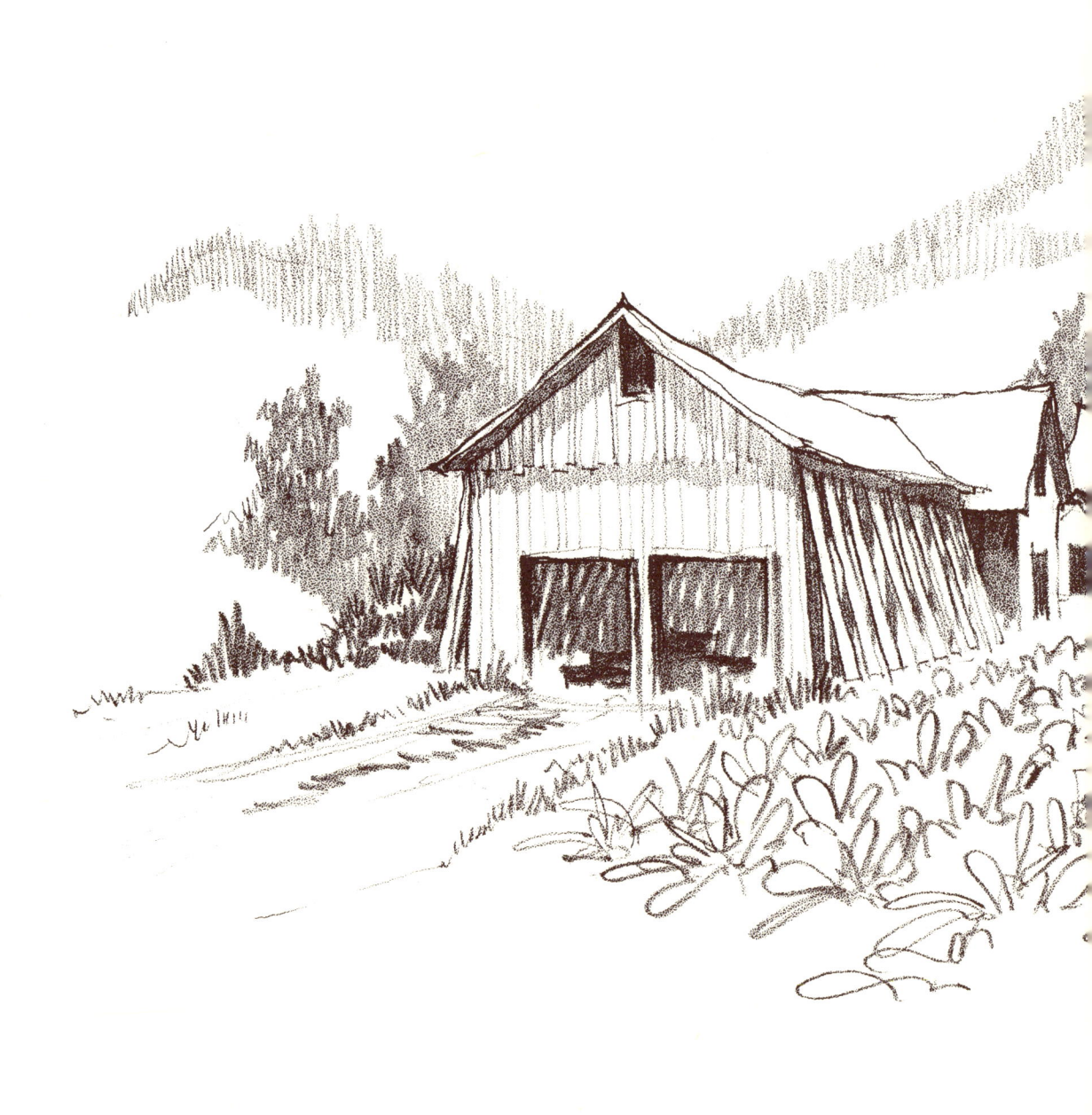

Tobacco-drying sheds below Mount Sugarloaf

Piano garden!—Whately

Tales of similar ambushes during King Philip's War are familiar in the area. The worst was the Bloody Brook Massacre on September 18, 1675, when seventy-six men out of a party of eighty-four carrying corn to the mill at Hadley were slaughtered by local Indians as they paused for refreshment by the side of a stream. Edward Everett Hale immortalized the incident in his famous poem "Bloody Brook."

It was nearby Deerfield, of course—one of New England's more popular "preserved villages"—that suffered most during this turbulent era of Indian insurgency. Following the Bloody Brook Massacre most of Deerfield's population moved farther south to better-protected communities in the valley. For almost a decade the place was a ghost town as even the hardiest of settlers gave it wide berth. Then, in 1682, the population began to return and all went well for a while—until Indian hostilities again erupted in the area. The 1702–13 Queen Anne's War led to Deerfield's second demise. In the great raid of 1704 most of the town was destroyed, and Deerfield's pastor, Reverend John Williams, along with 110 other inhabitants, was force-marched by the Indians into Canada. Although Williams survived the ordeal to describe his experiences in his book *The Redeemed Captive,* there were many groups, from all parts of western New England, who were subjected to similar marches and who were far less fortunate.

Peace finally came to this troubled community following the signing of a treaty with the Indians in 1735. The majority of the well-preserved homes that line the long, tree-shaded main street date from that period.

Today Pioneer Valley is a quiet, prosperous corner of northern Massachusetts. With the exception of Deerfield, most of its villages are not subjected to the regular onslaught of tourism. Hatfield, Whately and, to some extent, Hadley are all charming communities boasting collections of Colonial and Victorian homes. These of course were originally farmhouses that lined the wide, shady main streets, and many of the old rear barns and sheds are still in existence. Whately in particular has some fine groupings at the northern end of the street, just past this delightful "piano garden" outside the home of an organ and piano salesman. However, it's out in the flat fields along the river that barn freaks will find the best examples. Scores of tobacco-drying sheds line the narrow roads or stand in isolated groups in the cloth-tented fields. During the drying period their hinged sides can be moved to control the flow of air through the buildings. On a bright day the shadow patterns formed by these open vents produce strange visual illusions, especially if one drives rapidly past a series of such buildings.

Many of the original settlers considered tobacco the Devil's weed, and its cultivation a major sin. Unlike their counterparts in Virginia, who used to purchase their blushing brides from Europe with tobacco (upwards of 120 pounds per bride), Pioneer Valley inhabitants raised the more staple crops of onions, potatoes and corn until early religious fervor wore off in favor of more pragmatic considerations. As the local farmers grew more wealthy, the ministers became more tolerant. One Whately pastor once made the remark that he "didn't particularly care what his parishioners raised if they would only raise his salary." In recent years, however, the importance of tobacco growing has diminished considerably in the valley, although connoisseurs still claim that the shade-grown Pioneer Valley leaves produce some of the finest cigar wrappers in the world, equaling or exceeding the highly prized Sumatra crop.

This beautiful stretch of the Connecticut Valley between Northampton and Greenfield has a remarkably unspoiled character. Farther north around Turners Falls industry creeps in, and there's a splendid view of old brick paper mills from the road above the falls. But for the most part the valley offers sweeping vistas of flat green fields set against a backcloth of the eastern Berkshires. Travelers on Route 91 rarely venture into the small towns or onto the narrow country roads following the river's curves, so it's normally very quiet—and that's just fine!

5. THE NORTHERN BERKSHIRES
The "Still Voice" of the Mountains

The hills and smooth valley fields of Cummington are best seen from the lawn of the William Cullen Bryant homestead. Way below is the village, snuggled in a corner of the valley, and in the distance the rolling Berkshires recede in gradations of soft green. It was here, at the age of eighteen, that Cullen, as he was called by his father, composed his finest poem, "Thanatopsis." Even though the great romantic lines may seem somewhat ponderous today, Bryant's understanding of nature—her power, her healing, her stillness—is impressive in its truth:

> To him who in the love of Nature holds
> Communion with her visible forms, she speaks
> A various language; for his gayer hours
> She has a voice of gladness, and a smile
> And eloquence of beauty, and she glides
> Into his darker musings, with a mild
> And healing sympathy, that steals away
> Their sharpness, ere he is aware. When thoughts
> Of the last bitter hour come like a blight
> Over thy spirit, and sad images

Bryant Homestead—near Cummington

> Of the stern agony, and shroud, and pall,
> And breathless darkness, and the narrow house,
> Make thee to shudder and grow sick at heart;-
> Go forth, under the open sky, and list
> To Nature's teachings, while from all around-
> Earth and her waters, and the depths of air-
> Comes a still voice:-

The area in which Bryant found his muse remains one of the most tranquil parts of the Berkshires. In contrast, the Housatonic region to the west has long been a fashionable enclave of culture buffs from the East Coast metropolitan areas. Its conscious rurality, its links with a vivid literary past, its festivals and "occasions," all create a contagious dynamism on the one hand, but a somewhat contrived environment on the other.

During the first half of the nineteenth century the Housatonic Valley became the showplace of enlightened liberalism. Mark Hopkins and F. A. P. Barnard were both products of its advanced concepts, and from the 1820s until the outbreak of the Civil War a literary "workshop" flourished from Lanesboro to Great Barrington that was unequaled in richness of output except possibly by the Charles River Group of Boston. Its headquarters for many years was Catharine Sedgwick's literary salon in Lenox. Through its elegantly furnished rooms passed some of the great names of American literature—Herman Melville, Oliver Wendell Holmes, Henry Wadsworth Longfellow, Jonathan Edwards, Nathaniel Hawthorne.

"Wall of wood"—near Peru

Today, within a very few miles of the Housatonic, travelers may still happily lose themselves in the narrow back roads that cross the Berkshires to the east. With a little careful planning and a good map, it's possible to travel the fifty or so miles from Huntington in the south to the Vermont border in the north without using a main highway. The river road through the Chesters to Peru is a particularly memorable drive—it was along here that I sketched this most unusual "wall of wood." Also, the rutted skyline trail from Hinsdale to Middlefield provides some fine glimpses of the rolling Berkshires.

The best mountain view, though, is from the green in Middlefield itself. Here's another of those villages once famous for its industry—in this instance the manufacture of woolen goods from locally raised Saxony sheep. Unfortunately the town's prosperity was terminated abruptly in 1874, when a disastrous flood destroyed the local dam and many of the factories. However, the hardy settlers were not discouraged and set about rebuilding Middlefield—only to have the sequence reoccur in 1901. This time no one attempted to rebuild the dam. Cattle were imported instead, and the village slowly became what it is today, a pastoral hilltop community with a few old homes, a general store, a church—and some of the most memorable vistas in western Massachusetts.

Few signs remain of the important part industry played in village economics during the mid-nineteenth century. For example, Plainfield, which can be reached along a beautiful narrow road from Cummington, was known throughout the Berkshires for its cider brandy and maple sugar. There was also a mill for making satinette, a broom handle factory, a number of nearby paper mills and a foundry, where Homan Hallock made typefaces for printing the Bible in Arabic. But again, little remains from the past except a rather pleasant grouping of buildings halfway down the steep main street.

Near the Vermont border, the communities along the North River Valley were famous for their iron works. Colrain was in addition a sheep-raising center prior to the Civil War. This pleasant village with its verandahed buildings was named by its early Northern Irish settlers after Baron Coleraine of Ireland, who, it is said, was so delighted with the idea of an American settlement having his name that he promised to send a huge bell for the local church. Unfortunately the bell never arrived, but the village retained the name even though its population during the early 1800s was almost entirely French Canadian. In fact it was 1934 before Colrain's Roman Catholic Church began conducting services in English.

Rarely do I offer "What to Avoid" warnings, but in the case of the Mohawk Trail section of Route 2, which crosses the region from North Adams to Greenfield, I make a special exception. The road itself, particularly where it follows the generous sweeps of the Deerfield River, provides some splendid vistas. However, these are invariably spoiled by the roadside junk—crudely designed tourist stores, cafes and even mini-amusement parks—randomly scattered along its length, and concentrated, most distasteful of all, just west of Greenfield on the edge of that

Main street—Colrain

Cascades above Hoosac Tunnel

superb descent from the mountains into the Connecticut Valley. Plastic wigwams, fiberglass totem poles and giant-size statues of Indian warriors holding sales signs have no place in this landscape. (Actually it's questionable whether they have a place anywhere outside Disney World!)

Fortunately escape from this garish commercial strip is not hard. Many unspoiled villages still exist, only a few miles from Route 2. Buckland, another hilltop community that was once the home of Mary Lyon, founder of Mount Holyoke College, is typical of the charm and simplicity of these crisp, white Berkshire communities.

The region also abounds in natural features of great beauty. The unmarked Sanderson Brook Falls are located a few miles to the west of Huntington on US 20. Although the steep drive up the rough path may be hard on the car, the view is well worth the journey—feathery cascades of water falling over a hundred feet to the stream in the valley below.

In the center of the region at West Chesterfield is the Chesterfield Gorge. Again directional signs are minimal, but this impressive piece of glacial sculpture through which a fast-running stream tumbles and churns is worth finding. Thirty years ago it was the home of Chandler Clarence Clayton Bicknell, better known as the "Nutshell Man," whose local gift shop was famous for its unusual trinkets and machines, all invented and manufactured by Mr. Bicknell. One elderly gentleman I met at the Gorge had known him well. He pulled out a worn pocketbook and showed me some old sepia prints of the tiny store and a series of postcards bearing Bicknell's poetry. One ditty began:

> In my motor car I sit,
> Thinking of life's many ills,
> Of the ways the dollars flit,
> And of unpaid auto bills.

It went on to describe the disillusionment of all auto owners and the advantages of an "old and lazy horse"!

Way up in the northwestern corner of this region is the Hoosac Tunnel, a remarkable feat of civil engineering, constructed in fits and starts between 1851 and 1875 and still active today. I mention it because—unknown to many of the railroad buffs who come here on weekends to drink their way through cartons of beer and watch the great locomotives burst out of the black hole in the side of the mountain—there's a beautiful walk up through the woods that starts right by the opening. It's steep, and parts have become overgrown, but eventually it leads to a deep pool fed by two cascades. It's always peaceful here, and the pool is a perfect place to bathe on a hot summer afternoon. The lines of Bryant's poem could well have been composed here—

> . . . from all around-
> Earth and her waters, and the depths of air-
> Comes a still voice:-

6. THE GREAT RHODE ISLAND SWAMP
The Massacre of the Narragansetts

It took many miles of circuitous driving before I found the entrance to the Great Swamp. I had caught fleeting glimpses of jungle-like vegetation and small ponds from the roads around its western edge, but the track leading to its heart was elusive.

Finally, having found it, I bumped down its rutted surface for a couple of miles before coming to a small clearing, where I parked the car. Then I walked—walked and walked along meandering footpaths through this strange, overgrown wilderness. Dead trees lay rotting in pools; new trees grew out of old ones still silhouetted against the sky; black, leafless limbs projected from trunks wrapped in thick green ivy. Bird calls broke the stillness. They sounded strangely hollow and disconnected—eerie echoes of invisible life. Occasional rustles and grunts came from the undergrowth, but these too were disembodied sounds. Nothing moved—no creature scuttled across my path, no bird flew between the trees. Even on that hot, bright summer afternoon I had a distinct prickly sensation in my spine, a butterfly or two in my stomach. I felt that every step I took deeper into the swamp was being observed by a thousand tiny eyes.

I remembered the sign in the clearing where I had left the car: STAY ON THE FOOTPATH. Already it had narrowed from a cart track to a thin gap between clumps of thick bushes and ferns. It twisted more and more; I found it hard to see where I was going and wondered if I had somehow left the main track and was about to lose myself in one of the swamp's many silent backwaters. It seemed to be getting darker. The sun was no longer visible through the trees so I had no idea in which direction I was walking. I wondered why I had ever decided to come so far when all I had needed was a little descriptive background. I felt lost and somewhat alarmed—but I certainly was getting the flavor of the place! By the time I eventually found my way back to the car, an hour or so later, the sad history of this area seemed very real to me.

The date was December 1675, and the Narragansett Indians must certainly have felt most secure in their winter camp deep in the heart of this swamp. A vicious war between New England settlers and Indian tribes led by Metacom had erupted in June of that year at Swansea, Massachusetts. Resentment had been growing over many decades. Although there were a few enlightened settlers, such as Rhode Island's founder, Roger Williams, who had been banished from the Massachusetts Bay Colony in 1636 for opposing the granting of Indian territory to the whites by royal charter, the Indians had been systematically duped and cheated out of most of their land and weapons. When Metacom claimed that his brother, Wamsutta, one of the leaders of the Wampanoags, had been murdered while imprisoned by the settlers, this was greeted by many of the tribes as but one more in a long series of acts of aggression and betrayal. Metacom immediately began to organize a vast alliance of tribes from the Delaware to Canada.

Later, as the inevitable confrontation drew closer, a special plea for peace by the governor of Massachusetts was turned down by Metacom, in a truly regal manner: "Your Governor is but a subject of King Charles of England. I shall not treat with a subject. I shall treat of peace only with the King, my brother. When he comes, I am ready." From that time onward Metacom became known as King Philip, "Brother of Kings," and the tribes of New England rose up together to rid themselves of their persecuters.

In the following months fifty-two of the ninety New England settlements were attacked. Thirteen were eradicated entirely (see "Hatfield and Vicinity"—page 25), more than a thousand settlers were killed and the economic stability of the colonies was wrecked. In the New Plymouth Colony alone, the cost of the war amounted to over $260,000—a vast sum in those days.

During the fall of 1675 it was rumored that the Narragansetts, until that time a friendly Rhode Island tribe, were about to join King Philip. While many local settlers disputed this assumption and refused to take up arms, a force of more than a thousand New Englanders was amassed to attack the Narragansetts at their winter camp in the Great Swamp, near Kingston, before they could organize for war. The massacre—there is no other word to describe this episode—took place on December 19 on the frozen ponds. More than two thousand Indians were slaughtered, many dying without weapons in their burning tents. This was undoubtedly the

Indian church—near Charlestown

Chimney room, Gilbert Stuart House
—near Kingston

turning point of the war, although King Philip continued to organize attacks until he was finally betrayed and shot by one of his own men in the swamp near Bristol in 1676. The war dragged on for a further two years, but the Indian tribes were eventually decimated, their culture smashed and their spirit broken.

Of course Indian problems continued to plague New England for another century during the long series of wars between France and England, but it was usually tribes from Canada and Maine who challenged the Yankee settlers. The southern New England tribes slowly vanished. Even the special reservation near Charlestown created for the remnant of the Narragansetts was sold in 1881. All that remains is a burial ground and, deep in the woods north of Charlestown, the simple Indian church, erected in 1859 to replace an earlier 1750 structure. Although there is a small sign marking the route to the church, most travelers miss it, or turn back when the track through the woods becomes too rough.

Fortunately this area abounds with more easily accessible points of interest. It's best to abandon all maps and set your course by the sun. There are few road signs, but the back roads are great fun and, even in this relatively urbanized state, totally natural.

To the south of the Great Swamp is Worden Pond, a place I visited on a summer evening after the weekend tourists had gone. Gently rolling hills enclose the lake on all sides, and its waters have a distinctive deep red color, apparently due to their high iron content. In my notes I described the lake as "limbo-like." I sat for a long time on one of the rocks at the water's edge, looking across its smooth surface. Distances were difficult to gauge, and the lake had a curiously hypnotic quality. There was a sense of utter peace in its stillness—in the soft outline of the hills and the silence that seemed to cocoon the surroundings. Doubtless I arrived at a fortuitous time; there was no one else to spoil that special tranquility.

Over to the east, past the attractive hilltop community of Kingston, is an old mill, birthplace of one of New England's best known eighteenth-century artists, Gilbert Stuart. This was in fact the first snuff mill in America, founded by Stuart's Scottish father, and it is still operated today for demonstration purposes. Gilbert seems to have spent much of his early life traveling between America, Scotland and Ireland, until he ran up enormous debts in the last country and returned to the States in 1793 to devote the rest of his life to painting portraits of the famous and the wealthy. By the time of his death in 1828 he was said to have produced well over a thousand works—of which at least 124, and possibly as many as 400, were of George Washington. He was an impetuous artist who rapidly tired of detail; his most famous Washington portrait remains only half completed.

The Stuart home is now an interesting museum of American domestic life during the late eighteenth century. Particularly fascinating is the "chimney room," a tiny space behind the main fireplace used for drying herbs and as a cozy children's playroom during the bitter New England winters.

Stuart's mill operated at a time when many communities in this part of Rhode Island were beginning to industrialize. Textile mills were particularly common here, many of them founded by English entrepreneurs who left their homeland in disgust during the early 1800s when the Luddite revolts slowed the pace of industrialization. Shannock became well known for its fabric webbing, and other nearby towns, such as Kenyon, Alton and Bradford, were all involved in various aspects of textile manufacture. Even today many of the mills are still in active operation.

Particularly interesting is Alton, a true mill town, where identically designed homes line both sides of a wide main street leading to the dam and the mill. As in England, the homes were all constructed by the mill owner, and the town has that quality of regimentation so common in the textile communities of Yorkshire and Lancashire and so unusual in the heart of the New England countryside.

Traveling through these towns, one cannot help but be impressed by the speed and ingenuity with which these early entrepreneurs developed their prosperous industrial base. One wonders what would have happened if their predecessors had failed to defeat the Narragansetts in the swamps of Rhode Island during that bitter winter of 1675 . . .

7. CUTTYHUNK ISLAND
A Place to Enjoy Your Own Company

Cuttyhunk is one of the Elizabeth Island chain that extends southwestward from Falmouth on Cape Cod. To the east is Martha's Vineyard; a few miles to the north, Buzzards Bay and the Massachusetts coast. Most of the islands are privately owned, and Cuttyhunk is the only one accessible from the mainland by public ferry.

I never intended to stay overnight on Cuttyhunk. I'd taken the boat from New Bedford in the morning and expected to spend three hours or so exploring the island before returning in the evening for one of those gargantuan seafood dinners at Louie's on the Wharf Restaurant. The day was all planned, and everything was going fine. The trip across on the little ferryboat was smooth but uneventful—except when a sack of potatoes rolled off the top of a pile of deck freight and almost smothered one of those highly strung, yelp-and-whine poodles. Its owner, a well-endowed matron with bleached hair and fluorescent pink-framed spectacles, made such a fuss that the harassed captain had to lock his wheelroom door from the inside and hide behind his charts for the rest of the voyage. Fortunately the experience silenced the poodle, and the creature cowered under the seat with an occasional nervous glance across at the boxes, drums and crates piled in a wobbly pyramid in the center of the deck.

It was only when I had completed my stroll around the island and was slowly sauntering back to the pier that the day started to go wrong. There was no ferryboat there—just a couple of rowboats and a rather lopsided

Beach scene—Cuttyhunk

fishing trawler with a broken mast. Then I looked across the harbor and out to sea. There she was, the little orange vessel *Alert,* chugging merrily past the headland on her return trip to New Bedford. Even during the peak of the summer tourist season there's only one ferry a day, and I'd missed it. So I was marooned until the following day—stuck on a little patch of sand and scrub way out in the Atlantic. Actually it's only about fourteen miles off the mainland, but that's far enough to give one a distinct sense of isolation—not to mention despair as I realized I would have to forego that seafood dinner at Louie's.

As it turned out, the extended stay proved to be one of the most pleasant interludes in my New England travels. I found a room at the delightfully homey Allen House, one of the two hotels on the island. I ate dinner family-style with the other guests—platter after platter of freshly caught bass cooked in sweet butter and herbs—and roamed every track and path through the thick, windswept scrub of sumac and bayberry. I chatted with the islanders and met some of the "year-rounders," a hearty bunch of forty or so individuals who live here permanently and, from what I could tell, make a living by doing odd jobs for one another or taking out amateur fishermen to hunt the great bass that run between the Elizabeth Islands. I heard from the "summerites"—who live here only during the warmer part of the year—of the age-old feuds between some of the year-rounders. "It's just like a soap opera," one summerite told me. "Every June I come back and I'm hardly off the boat before they start giving me the rundown of winter escapades. For the first week my house is never empty. There's always someone coming in with tales—fantastic tales—about the goings-on here. And they get so serious—there're some families that never speak to one another. Still, what can you expect, it's a tiny place, most of the homes are all bunched up together, and forty people with nothing to do for six months—well, it's amazing there aren't annual massacres."

Out in the scrub beyond the village are deer, a herd of fifty or so. At first I didn't believe it, since there are no trees, no woods for them to hide in. I thought I was being told one of those island folktales—like the story of the ghost in the great Forbes family mansion on Nashawena Island across the bay. As it turned out I was wrong. Before breakfast, in fact just around dawn, I took a stroll up the hill, out of the village and deep into the undulating wilderness of the island. There were no sounds except for the distant rush of the surf up the rocky beaches. The dew was heavy and glistened on the leaves of the bushes. Occasionally the path would pass over a hillet from which I could see the tall stone tower in the lagoon at the end of the island, but for the most part it meandered through the thick scrub, full of the fresh aroma of morning. I spotted a rabbit, a large one, just ahead. It saw me too, but didn't pay much attention and resumed its leafy breakfast. I walked right up to it, and still it continued its nibbling. When I put my hand out to stroke it, the creature stopped eating, gave me a look of annoyance for interrupting its meal and waited for me to withdraw my hand. I did, and it resumed breakfast with complete indifference to my presence.

It was then I saw the deer. He must have watched the little incident with the rabbit, for there was no fear in the way he stood—in fact there seemed to be a distinct gleam of amusement in his eyes. Having decided I was absolutely harmless, he began advancing toward me, occasionally flicking his magnificent head with its three-foot-long antlers. I started to back off, and felt rather stupid. He was supposed to back off from *me*—it says so in all the books: "The deer is a timid creature. . . ." Fortunately after a few yards he got bored and started nibbling bayberry leaves, and I was able to resume my walk. By the time I arrived back in the village I had seen at least six full-grown deer, one fawn, three more rabbits and a snake (the island variety is apparently harmless). I saw my final deer—a beautiful beige doe—enjoying a hearty breakfast of chrysanthemums in a garden near the hotel. Even the high fence, a common sight around many of the village homes, had failed to keep her out.

It is memories like these that make Cuttyhunk such a special place. There was the old fisherman from Finland, sitting outside his tiny wooden shack shucking clams for a chowder. On one of the tracks leading out of the village was a sign typical of the spirit of the island: **YOU ARE NOW ENTERING PRIVATE LANDS. WELCOME.** The inhabitants, for all their supposed feuding, are friendly and seem to enjoy the handful of tourists who arrive daily during the summer to stroll the narrow paths and tan on the white beaches. One woman spent half an hour answering my questions about the island's history and even invited me to join her family for dinner.

I remember too the complete lack of commercialism. There are no hot dog stands, and just one small village store, up the hill from the harbor. The homes are simple New England structures, Cape Cods and saltboxes. There's no liquor on the island—it's totally dry; the two public phones operate on the party line system and still have crank handles for contacting the operator. I made one call to the mainland; it was accidentally disconnected twice, interrupted half a dozen times by other party

Typical island footpath—Cuttyhunk

liners (one of whom actually joined in on the conversation), and finally terminated in a barrage of static, which I believe was a not too subtle hint from the operator that she considered my time to be up.

This tiny, unspoiled blob of land could have become one of New England's most historic sites, for it was here that Bartholomew Gosnold and his thirty-two-man crew landed on May 25, 1602, intending to start a colony, possibly for Sir Walter Raleigh. The stone tower at the western end of the island, built in 1903, marks the site of the first English habitation on the coast of New England. According to Gosnold's records, there were exuberant celebrations that led inevitably to overindulgence: "The powder of sassafras in twelve hours cured one of our company that had taken a great surfeit by eating the bellies of dogfish, a very delicious meat."

It was this sassafras, covering the island, that sealed the fate of the little colony. It appears that Gosnold was not particularly trusted by his crew, for when he proposed to return to England with a valuable cargo of sassafras, leaving behind most of his men, there was almost instant rebellion. Gosnold assured them he intended to make a lucrative sale, buy fresh supplies and return early the following year to the island. He almost persuaded them, and many of the crew began to lay out a plantation as Gosnold went off to explore another island in the Elizabeth chain. But unfortunately he didn't return when expected, and food supplies on Cuttyhunk ran out. One of the sailors, Gabriel Archer, wrote in his diary that the men were "in a dumpish terror" and were obliged to live on "alexander and sorrel pottage, ground nuts and tobacco." To make matters worse a member of the crew was wounded by Indians who were angered that Gosnold had stolen one of their canoes.

Transportation on Cuttyhunk!

When Gosnold finally came back a few days later, the crew had rejected all ideas of plantations and colonies. They chose instead to sail home to ensure they received their share of the sassafras profits—and the island was abandoned.

During the great whaling years of the nineteenth century Cuttyhunk became the headquarters for many of the navigational pilots who guided the ships through the narrows between the islands and into New Bedford. In 1864 the exclusive Cuttyhunk Club was founded as a center for the rich man's sport of bass fishing, and in 1921 William Wood, owner of the vast American Woolen Company, took over the club's interests and even attempted to buy up the whole island for use as a private resort. His attempt failed, but he went ahead and constructed the huge stone mansion that still towers above the village, looking rather out of place among the little gray and white cottages. Just below the mansion is another Wood creation, the rambling Avalon Club. Owned until recently by Frank Sinatra's theatrical agent, it is today in need of considerable refurbishment.

Cuttyhunk really is a little world unto itself. It's not on the New England tourist route, possibly because there's not much to do there except enjoy the peace of its quiet lanes and match wits with the occasional deer. There are few cars or trucks because of the lack of paved roads and places to go. However, there are some remarkable vehicular artifacts, many of which still manage to sputter a few hundred yards if necessary. This was one of my favorites.

Essentially, Cuttyhunk is what you make of it. If you enjoy your own company, you'll love it.

Region II:
Vermont and
New Hampshire

8. MONADNOCK AND THE SOUTHERN LAKES
A Kingdom of the Muse

"Come on, y'all know Dick Mossley. This is Dick's crib, Dick's very own crib, folks . . . why, when he was just a little baby, Dick used to chew these wooden bars . . . well, it's either that or woodworm . . ." The crowd chuckles. "Now we're gonna start on a dollar. Who's gonna be the one to get the ball rollin'. C'mon now, we've got a lot of stuff to get rid of here. Reverend! Hey! Reverend! Finish talkin' fishin' . . . and you, Tom, leave the Reverend alone. Now, one dollar, Reverend? One dollar it is. One-fifty, two, two-fifty, c'mon now, it's in fine condition . . . three. Hey! Mary Rose, why you biddin'? Heeeo! I didn't know you needed a crib! What have you been up ta, Mary Rose? Hey! Ken, you been seein' Mary Rose lately? Now, Mary Rose, you come back here, Mary Rose . . ."

Great ripples of laughter come from the crowd gathered on the village green at Jaffrey Center as poor Mary Rose tries to hide her blushes. She knows them all, they all know her—and everyone's having fun at the church sale on a hot afternoon. Some of the young kids of the village are selling homemade lemonade, and under the shade trees a group of housewives is running the cake-and-cookie table. And there, out in the middle of the green, is the auctioneer, one of the villagers, just having the time of his life—cracking jokes, embarrassing the girls and selling off a huge pyramid of baby carriages, televisions, lamps, coatracks, washing machines, great stuffed chairs, even a maple sap boiler and an ancient cast iron furnace.

It was a beautiful summer afternoon. I lay around for an hour or more drinking lemonade, nibbling cookies and watching the scene: a village community at play. I could have stayed all day. I was utterly exhausted,

Monadnock, view from the south

having just completed an early morning climb of nearby Mount Monadnock, New Hampshire's "airy citadel." I arrived at the bald, wind-torn summit long before the daily crowd had even begun the two-hour climb, and watched the sun rise through the morning mist that lay lightly over the wooded land below. All of New England's six states were visible; way in the distance, a hundred miles to the north, was the vague outline of Mount Washington. I could even distinguish the Berkshires to the west and, to the south, the Woonsocket Hills of Rhode Island.

Monadnock. Even the name has a power to it. Its somber beauty, its proud, masculine outline and its windy summit of white rock, all are known and loved today by the people of the southern lakes region, just as they were a century ago by the writers and artists who congregated around its base.

From the shores of Walden Pond, Thoreau could see the mountain's great bulk thrust up out of the plains and silhouetted against the sky. He wrote of it often and was known to have made the climb to the summit at least three times. In contrast to many of today's lightly equipped hikers, Thoreau always traveled with a full pack when he went on one of his nature walks. For example, on an 1860 tour-day hike up the mountain he carried, in addition to the more usual spare clothing, "umbrella, rubber coat, night cap, 'three bosoms' [white false shirt fronts "to go and come in"], spyglass, microscope, tape measure, saw, hatchet, blotting paper and twine and a small bag stuffed with moss for a pillow." This in addition to "two and one-half pounds of salt beef and tongue, eighteen hard-boiled eggs, two and one-half pounds of sugar, a quarter-pound of tea, two pounds of hard bread, half a loaf of home made bread and a piece of cake." He was indeed a well-provided man.

The nearby hilltop community of Dublin with its lovely pond was briefly spotlighted by a minor gold discovery in 1875, and a few years later became the center of a small colony of artists, including Alexander James (son of the philosopher William James); George de Forest Brush, famous for his series of mother-and-child portraits, and Abbott Thayer, best known for his work "Winter Sunrise, Monadnock." Although the village is still popular with artists, it is perhaps best known as the headquarters of *Yankee* magazine, the pleasant offices of which are located opposite the Dublin Library, which was the first free library in New Hampshire.

But it was the writers, rather than the artists, who painted the finest pictures of Monadnock and created its richest and most romantic images. The following quotations are but a few examples of the impact of the mountain on some of America's best-loved authors.

Mark Twain:

> From the base of the long slant of the mountain the valley spreads away to the circling frame of the hills, and beyond the frame the billowy sweep of remote great ranges rises to view and flows, fold upon fold, wave upon wave, soft and blue and unworldly, to the horizon fifty miles away. . . . Monadnock and the valley and its framing hills . . . are sumptuously splashed, mottled and betorched from skyline to skyline, with the richest dyes the Autumn can furnish.

Nathaniel Hawthorne:

> A sapphire close against the sky.

Ralph Waldo Emerson, in his poem "Monadnoc" (one of twenty known spelling variations):

> With inward fires and pain, it rose a bubble from the plain [presumably referring to its volcanic origin].

Rudyard Kipling:

> Monadnock came to mean everything that was helpful, healing and full of quiet and when I saw him half across New Hampshire he did not fail.

Somehow it seems most appropriate that the composer Edward MacDowell and his wife Marion, a well-known pianist, chose to establish the famous MacDowell Colony for writers, musicians and artists at Peterboro, only a few miles east of the great mountain. The colony, formally established in 1908 after the composer's death, is open to the public, and those who make a leisurely visit to the estate may sense the unique character of this region—a kingdom of the muse.

In contrast, many of the small towns to the north of the mountain were frantic industrial communities at the same time the great authors were writing their languid lines. Harrisville is a particularly interesting and attractive example of an early-nineteenth-century mill village. Situated at the southern end of a superb stretch of water known as Harrisville Pond, the town initially obtained its power from the rapids and falls linking this

Harrisville

pond with one below. This power operated the machinery used to produce woolen goods by all those strange-sounding processes—scouring, picking, carting, pulling, dyeing, napping, shearing, warping and a dozen other "ings" in between.

Industrial progress, even in these idyllic surroundings, was not without its problems. The town's main mill owner, Milan Harris, was a temperance-minded man, and when a group of Irish immigrants moved in during the mid-1800s he wrote in his journal that they had a "demoralizing influence on the village."

Poor Milan. Things went from bad to worse, and the 1856 records of the Congregational church state, rather forlornly, that "in consequence of the increasing numbers of foreigners who find employment in the factories, and other influences hostile to the welfare of Zion, the morals of the place cannot be said to compare favorably with what they were ten or fifteen years since."

In November of the same year, during the Frémont/Buchanan presidential race, Democrats in the village rioted against the emergence of the Republican Party; according to a local newspaper Milan and his factory were even fired upon by cannons. Somehow, though, he kept his business going and made a fortune producing uniforms during the Civil War. However, in 1874, at the age of seventy-five, he lost his fortune equally rapidly and sold the mill to local competitors, thereafter passing on into history.

Today Harrisville is a well-preserved place rich in brick and stone architecture, much of it in the Charles Bulfinch tradition. The view of the northern part of the village, with its church reflected in Harrisville Pond, is one of the most naturally photogenic scenes in New Hampshire.

A second onetime industrial community to the north reflects the region's famous tradition of glassmaking. Stoddard, a tiny hillside community, and its adjoining hamlets boasted three factories during their prime, whose glassblowers were almost as well known as their products. They had a remarkable capacity for liquor after a hard day's work, and the now extinct Gilson's Tavern in South Stoddard had doors wide enough to permit a man on horseback to ride up to the bar, and a fireplace so large that oxen were occasionally used to drag the great logs through the door and right under the chimney.

Well cover—Nelson

Glassmaking began here in 1842, when Joseph "Old Bottle" Foster left his position as chief blower at a Keene factory and started a small works on the flat below Stoddard. Others followed, and the area soon became known for its eight-sided ink bottles, liquor flasks, wicker-covered one-gallon wine demijohns—and also for its "end-of-day" articles—miscellaneous creations by the blowers that were often distributed by Yankee peddlers and later became treasured collector's items.

Unfortunately glass manufacturing in the area was short-lived. Many of the Keene factories were obliged by the strict local temperance societies

Hancock

to curtail production of their well-known green and amber liquor bottles. Plants at Stoddard and also those in other communities, such as the beautiful hilltop village of Temple to the southeast, began to close around the time of the Civil War, when a combination of economic depression and an increasing demand for clear glass, made production unprofitable.

Two other settlements in this lake-dotted region are well worth a visit. The village of Nelson is located on a hilltop a few miles north of Harrisville. In addition to this ornate well cover that sits in the middle of the green, there's a most attractive church complete with the rear sheds where horse-drawn buggies and carriages were once parked during Sunday services. It is claimed by many historians that one of the ways in which strangers used to gauge the prosperity of an area was by the condition and quality of the carriages in these church sheds on Sunday mornings.

To the east of Harrisville, along some of the prettiest back roads in the lake country, is the tranquil and dignified community of Hancock. The place seems totally unaffected by the passage of time, although at one point in its history it was one of New Hampshire's main cotton manufacturing centers. Today little remains of that era, and instead visitors enjoy this delightful bandstand scene at the lower end of the village by the finely detailed Congregational church, or visit the interesting Historical Society Museum on the main street, not far from the picturesque Norway Pond.

Main street—Bellows Falls

9. BELLOWS FALLS
An Interesting Example of Townscape

Bellows Falls? A hidden corner? Well, since the opening of Interstate 91 the town has become a relatively quiet place, unfrequented by most visitors to the region. It's an industrial community possessing few of the pristine charms of the Vermont and New Hampshire hill towns, yet it has a distinctively attractive quality.

There are only a handful of towns along the northern section of the Connecticut River that reflect its turbulent past as New England's main link between the coast and the mountainous hinterland. Although Brattleboro and Windsor both have that flavor of sturdy brick-and-stone permanence, the most interesting community is without doubt Bellows Falls. Very few towns in New England—with the possible exception of Manchester, New Hampshire—combine industrial character with those qualities of urban form usually found in old European cities.

Take a stroll on Westminster Street, the main thoroughfare of Bellows Falls, as it winds along a narrow ledge of rock between the steep drop to the river below and an even more abrupt rise to the one fashionable residential area, overlooking the valley. Although the stores have a rather seedy appearance and the once proud town hall with its Florentine tower has recently been converted into a cinema, the tight, twisting space of the street provides a subtle articulation of townscape rarely found in American communities. The tower, for example, as seen from the northern end of Westminster Street acts as a fulcrum for the abrupt change in direction of the road—a kind of elaborate pivot that is also a dominant element of the town's "square." The interesting thing about this space is that it is not the standard *square* square, rigidly defined on some nineteenth-century city planner's drawing board. Rather the street just happens to widen at the point of maximum activity and the vista is closed, first, by a group of buildings at the far end, and more dramatically by the rocky mass of Mount Kilburn, which broods over the town on the opposite side of the river.

It has all the spatial flavor of an old Italian hill town. Watch for the narrow gaps between the buildings that provide brief glimpses, not just of more buildings, but of the woods and fields on the other side of the valley, a shimmer of sunshine on the river and bright blue sky against the grimy brick and dark stairways in the alleys. Look also for the steep steps that make an abrupt though attractive link between Westminster and School Streets. To capture the real drama of the town setting, stroll out past the unusual Spanish-style post office (the blueprints must have been mixed up—this design is pure "Santa Barbara") across the bridge and over the rapids. In spring the white water churns around the right-angled bend in the river, smashing against the scarred rock banks before tumbling under the bridge and out through a narrow chasm into the wide and relatively placid stretch below. During the summer the scene is a little more tranquil. The level of the water then is low, and the drama of the spring flood can only be guessed at by studying the torn, bleached rocks in the streambed.

Street scenes—Bellows Falls

The falls, during summer—Bellows Falls

These notorious rapids were one of the main obstacles to opening up effective trade links with the hinterland of northern New England. So in 1792 a British-owned company began construction of a canal, the first such attempt in America. This complex engineering feat required nine locks and ten years of continuous labor to complete. Its opening in 1802 enabled lumber to be floated downstream—at least that portion of the lumber not consumed by Bellows Falls' huge paper mills. It was here that William Russell, later president of the International Paper Company, developed some of the first successful methods for producing paper from wood pulp, which later were to make the town one of the most important paper-producing centers in the nation.

The real glory days of the canal came with the steamboats during the 1820s and '30s. Advertisements and flyers proclaimed a new era of travel: **THE CONNECTICUT RIVER—THE GRAND HIGHWAY FROM CANADA TO THE SEABOARD**. "Give us steam! Give us steam!" was the motto and the toast. Occasionally there was too much steam: more than one vessel had a boiler explode as it churned up through the fast-flowing waters to reach the first lock of the canal. There were other examples of overexuberance during this frantic period. The sidewheeler *William Hall,* for instance, arrived at the falls only to find it was too big to pass through the locks. Rather than turn back to the jeers of the crowd, the captain valiantly hired a team of oxen and had the boat towed through the streets to the top end of the canal, where it was relaunched to sail on to Hartland, near Windsor.

The canal era was short-lived. By the late 1840s, railroads had superseded river transport along the northern Connecticut, and Bellows Falls began to expand its industrial base, which during the middle of the century included the production of fine silk, developed in specially nurtured mulberry groves. Although these have long since disappeared, destroyed in the severe winter of 1845, many of the elaborate Victorian villas—homes of the wealthier merchants and entrepreneurs—remain on the bluff above the river. It was here, at the corner of School and Westminster Streets, that Hetty Green, the "Witch of Wall Street," lived for many years after she married a rich Bellows Falls businessman. Henrietta Howland Robinson Green managed her husband's and her own substantial investments in Wall Street with a wizardry that verged on the diabolical. She never made an unwise decision, and was one of the few financiers to predict the crash of 1907. For the last decade of her life she was known as the richest woman in America—and, according to local stories, one of the meanest!

In contrast to the bold urbanity of Bellows Falls is the village of Walpole, a short distance to the south, founded in 1752 by Colonel Benjamin Bellows under a grant from Governor Benning Wentworth. The water trough at its northern edge is a memorial to the long association of the Bellows family with the community. Walpole has all the distinctive characteristics of the dignified New England country town. Large white Colonial and Victorian/Gothic mansions sit in manicured gardens behind rows of old elm trees. There's a spacious green surrounded by churches (the community boasts a remarkable number of churches), two old inns that are now private residences and a well-kept cemetery, resting place of several of Colonel Bellows' sons. Regrettably none of the residences are open to the public. In fact the town does little to encourage tourists; the inhabitants seem to value their privacy. Nonetheless this is a rewarding and highly recommended side trip from Bellows Falls.

Bellows Trough—Walpole

Main street—Chester

10. CHESTER AND VICINITY
The Curious Legend of Clarence Adams

There can be few more endearing villains in New England history than Clarence Adams. His family was one of the most highly respected in Chester and was related directly to Presidents John Adams and John Quincy Adams. As befitted such a name, Clarence was first selectman of the community and a great advocate of law and order.

In September 1886 there began a series of mysterious burglaries in the town that continued unchecked for sixteen years. Most stores were robbed at least once, and poor James Pollard's General Store was raided a total of sixteen times during the period. The local miller, Charles Waterman, was also a regular victim.

Clarence Adams was always ready with ingenious schemes to capture the burglar, and even offered his own reward of $100 in addition to the official sum of $500. But somehow it made no difference—it was as though the burglar knew in advance of all schemes to catch him red-handed. Whenever the miller, for example, hired a watchman, usually on the advice of Clarence, the burglar never appeared. As soon as the watchman was considered unnecessary and let go, the unfortunate miller would lose another few bags of flour.

It all came to a head in 1902. The miller noticed that the burglar used a different entrance each time to gain access to the mill. Only one window remained that had not been used. So Mr. Waterman rigged up a shotgun trap at that particular window. If the lower pane was pried open, the burglar would trip the trigger and receive a generous blast of buckshot. For a week or two nothing happened. Then one night, the miller heard the long-awaited roar and rushed to the window—only to find the burglar gone with nothing but a pool of blood left behind. A thorough search of the area around the mill revealed no wounded villain, but the following morning it was rumored in the community that Mr. Adams had been wounded by a highwayman just outside town. This was too much of a coincidence for the miller, and he went snooping around the Adams farm as the poor gentleman lay writhing upstairs having shot removed from his lower limbs. Eventually the miller found all the evidence he needed, including several marked bags of flour. Poor Mr. Adams was arrested for burglary and sentenced to ten years in the state prison at Windsor. His last remarks as he was led away expressed the plight of an imaginative man forced to live according to dull social expectations: "What I have done, I attribute to the spirit of adventure that was born in me. I craved some excitement, something to occupy my mind aside from humdrum affairs."

Had the story ended there, it would have been amusing and slightly sad but nothing more. But subsequent events made Clarence Adams something of a legend in the area. It seems that after serving two years of his sentence he died suddenly, in March 1904. As it was still winter and the ground frozen, his coffined body was placed in a vault until the spring thaw, when his grave could be dug. However, in April reports reached his jailers that he'd been spotted traveling in Canada, first in Nova Scotia and then around Vancouver. The Hearst newspapers got hold of the story and pushed it for all it was worth. Reports came in from "Adams spotters" all over the continent. To make matters more confusing, although no one could say for certain, the body in the reopened coffin bore little resemblance to the mysterious Clarence. Even today the whole affair is still unexplained—although what really happened would likely be far less interesting than the legend!

Chester itself is today a well-preserved community. The central part, around the stores, has a distinct Victorian flavor, as the sketch shows, and the long, tree-lined main street provides an almost encyclopedic array of architectural styles popular during the late 1800s—Gothic, Stick and Shingle, Italianate, Classical Revival and a few odd specimens that attempt to combine all such influences into the "Conglomerate" vernacular—quite common on the West Coast but rare in conservative New England.

The churches of Chester are particularly notable. The brick Baptist church (1835) is situated at the edge of the town cemetery with its ominous "Public Tomb," a remnant of the days when bodies were stored during the winter for spring burial. Not far away is the large Congregational church (1829), a masterly piece of architecture boasting a five-tier tower obviously derived from the earlier works of the famous Boston

Porch scene—Chester

architect Charles Bulfinch. Nearby was the residence of Parson Flagg, yet another one of Chester's notable characters, who encouraged eloping couples, particularly those from New Hampshire, to have their marriage vows sanctified in his home—which rapidly gained notoriety as the Yankee equivalent of Scotland's Gretna Green.

Across from the cemetery, just below the stores, is the headquarters of the National Survey Company, a mapmaking firm cited for the accuracy of its products during World War II and still well known for its topographical maps, most of which are for sale in a nearby warehouse. The accompanying sketch of a secluded porch with its wicker rocking chairs was made down one of Chester's quiet side streets, and reflects that gentle pace of life for which New England is so well loved. To complete the idyllic atmosphere of this delightful village there is the fine old Chester Inn on the village green, which offers excellent accommodations and a splendid, inexpensive buffet lunch.

A mile or so down the road from Chester Depot, past the old fire station with its tall mansard-roofed tower, is a most unusual feature: a whole village constructed entirely of stone. Although occasional stone buildings are not uncommon in this part of Windsor County—there are a few scattered examples along Chester's main street—nowhere else is there a grouping such as this, with its superb architectural unity and detailed craftsmanship. Most of the homes and the church were constructed during the mid-1800s by the Clark brothers from Vermont. They had learned the stonemason's trade from Scottish experts in Canada and were highly respected in the region for their skill and speed. They were also noted for their remarkable consumption of rum. In addition to their $5-a-week wage they were provided with a gallon of the finest blend, which may well explain the speed with which many of these homes were erected!

To the south of Chester are a number of meandering country roads, usually partly paved, leading to such villages as Windham, Athens and Grafton. The last, though it has become rather commercialized in recent years, is a remarkable example of a restored New England community, thanks to the effort of Matthew Hall, his cousin, Dean Mathey, of Princeton University, and the nonprofit Windham Foundation. They, together with many of Grafton's residents, transformed the crumbling village into a thriving place of craft shops and galleries. They also restored the Old Tavern, which during the late 1800s was a regular gathering for the Boston literary set, including a host of notables such as Emerson, Thoreau and Kipling, and later was frequented by Presidents Theodore Roosevelt and Woodrow Wilson. It's a fine place to dine or, even better, to stay overnight, with a dawn stroll through the quiet, misty streets just as the countryside is waking up.

Stone village—Chester

Covered bridge—Townshend

Continuing southward past one of the most beautiful covered bridges in the region, the Scott Bridge near West Townshend, the roads join to pass through the hillside village of Townshend with its impressively ornate town hall dominating a street of Victorian Gothic villas, and down into what many visitors regard as one of southern Vermont's most delightful towns, Newfane. During the peak of the tourist season Newfane can lose some of its "hidden" quality as its two fine French restaurants attract considerable evening trade. The best time to visit is in the early spring or in the heart of fall, when the red and bronze foliage provides a superb backcloth for the crisp white buildings surrounding the large greens. The sketch shows three of the finest structures. On the left is Union Hall, the town hall (1832), originally erected as a church; behind is the delicately spired Congregational church (1839); to the right a most elaborate building—one of Vermont's most popular photographic subjects—the county courthouse (1825) with its splendid four-pillar portico. Just off the sketch is one of the oldest buildings in the town, the Newfane Inn (1793), which contains one of the French restaurants.

It was here in Newfane that Eugene Field, poet and author, spent much of his youth—though the town is perhaps more famous as the place with the "hotel jail." Rather than go to the effort of providing two sets of accommodations and dining facilities, one for petty criminals and the other for county court officials and other visitors, the canny Newfaners combined them in a building that still stands today across the street from the courthouse. In this way jailers, prisoners, clerks, witnesses and attorneys could all enjoy one another's company before proceeding to more serious business in the courthouse. Just one more example of unusual goings-on in the Green Mountains region of Vermont!

Newfane

11. THE SUTTONS TO WASHINGTON
A Brief but Beautiful Drive

Linking the northern lakes of New Hampshire, around Canaan, to the southern lake area between Stoddard and Mount Monadnock is this beautiful drive along back roads between the communities of North Sutton and Washington.

Kesar Lake is located at the northern end of the drive in Wadleigh State Park at North Sutton. This is one of my favorite lakes for swimming in New Hampshire, and the beach, just off the green, is particularly pleasant. An old hotel, now a collection of apartments, sits sedately on its landscaped lawn in front of a little white church. Children splash and play on the floating jetty and the water in the shallow bay always seems warm. It's only the irritating mosquitoes, big with blood, that spoil the otherwise idyllic atmosphere!

The narrow road passes southward through Sutton and South Sutton (birthplace of the Pillsbury brothers, founders of the nation's largest flour business), to the town of Bradford. Thanks to the main road bypass its quiet streets have maintained their charm, although the place still has plenty of life. I particularly remember one visit when the green by the side of the white church was packed with locals, clapping, cheering and

The beach—North Sutton

singing to the strains of a Veterans Brass Band. This was no ordinary band with a limited repertoire of marches and patriotic melodies. Led by the fiery conductor, it romped through Rodgers and Hammerstein themes, swung with old Glenn Miller favorites, blasted away at Sousa, attempted a Beethoven piece, followed by Ferde Grofé—and finally for good measure ended with a couple of rock-flavored Beatle tunes. A remarkable and unexpected performance!

After leaving Bradford by the covered bridge, the road meanders through woods and rolling hills to East Washington. From that point southward there's a latticework of back roads, some of which end abruptly in farmyards, others somehow coalescing to lead through the strange rocky landscape to Washington. I could find no satisfactory explanation for the preponderance of great boulders littering the fields and hillsides of this area. One farmer said he'd read it was all glacial rubble, left behind when the great ice sheets that once covered New England receded. Another told me a fantastic folktale about giants who apparently passed the time aiming these rocky missiles at each other with slingshots as big as trees. A third took me out into one of his back meadows and showed me that these great boulders had seemingly been arranged in unusual groupings of circles and crescents over the hillside. He thought it must have been the work of Indians who used to populate this area before the coming of the white settlers in the mid-seventeenth century. However, I could draw no final conclusions from what I heard—although the story of the giants really appealed!

Just outside the delightful hilltop village of Washington is a roadside plaque commemorating the founding of the Seventh Day Adventist Church here in April 1842, when a band of local citizens formed a First Christian Society. Later they erected a church in the woods, well away from the village, where they were able to worship without fear of persecution by conformist township residents.

It is interesting to realize just how many new religious sects began in New Hampshire and in adjoining Vermont. I've already discussed the emergence of Shaker communities (see "The Dale of Tyringham"—page 20); New Hampshire still possesses two remnants of this movement. The first, an extremely well-preserved museum village, is located a few miles east of Interstate 93, north of Concord. The second, now a Roman Catholic seminary, is alongside Mascoma Lake near Lebanon (see "Canaan and the Northern Lakes"—page 86). However, during the 1800s the region was a hotbed of other bizarre spiritually oriented groups, such as the Dorrelites, who followed a British army deserter said to possess supernatural powers, and the Pilgrims, founded by a self-styled prophet, Isaac Boullard, who led his group of disciples from the villages around Woodstock in search of a promised land in the West. Hardwick, a small town in Caledonia County in Vermont, also boasted its own sect during the 1830s, the New Lights. Members rejected the then popular Universalist form of service to create their own more demonstrative ceremony, in which, according to local records, rolling on the floor played an important part. Although the Hardwick minister, Reverend Chester Wright, attempted to show tolerance, he and his congregation eventually tired of these "Holy Roller" antics and had most of the group arrested for disturbing the peace, which effectively terminated their exuberance forever.

One of the few sects to endure was led by John Humphrey Noyes, a close relative of President Rutherford Hayes and an ordained minister—at least until he founded a religion based on the perfectionist philosophy in Putney, a busy little town on the Vermont side of the Connecticut Valley north of Brattleboro. At that point his statements became a little too excessive for the Congregational Church. Noyes claimed to be a brother of Jesus Christ and stressed the religious importance of unrestrained sexual relationships within his group, based on the concept of "complex marriage." The local populace became so incensed by his preaching that he was obliged to leave Putney rather hastily in October 1847.

His followers joined him in New York State, where they founded the Oneida Community. The practice of complex marriage was abandoned "in deference to public sentiment," and Oneida became an impressive example of a cooperative community based on agriculture and the manufacture of simple household products.

Without doubt the most durable of all these nineteenth-century groups was the Church of Christ, Scientist, founded by Mary Baker Eddy in 1879. Her birthplace at Bow, New Hampshire, just south of Concord, is

A boulder field—near Bradford

Washington

still preserved, and her complex personality remains the subject of much biographical debate. Nevertheless, unlike most of the short-lived Vermont and New Hampshire religions, the movement continues to flourish.

Before leaving the region for the southern lake country, it's worth pausing to explore Washington, one of the highest villages in the state and the second in the nation to take the President's name in 1776. Actually the inhabitants claim it was the first, and have erected a large sign to this effect near the green, but according to my information that honor resides with the community of Washington in Beaufort County, North Carolina.

This New Hampshire village, with its fine churches and bandstand, could easily become an artist's paradise. There are so many cameos of New England life around here—old barns with flaking red paint, a porch with rocking chair, shadows of old elm trees on white-painted wooden walls, a country lane meandering off across the green.

Most beautiful of all is the tiny Adventist church mentioned earlier. Follow the narrow road by the side of the bandstand down a series of long, steep hills. After about three miles there's a small hand-lettered sign nailed to a tree pointing along a rough track to the left. A little way down, set in a sunny clearing, sits the church with its simple white wooden facade. It's a lovely, silent place to rest awhile, to enjoy the sounds of the forest and the quiet pulse of life in this little-known corner of New Hampshire.

Farm machine?—near Washington

12. CLAREMONT
Elaborate Urbanity in a Pastoral Setting

Claremont, like Bellows Falls, can hardly be listed as a major tourist attraction. Nonetheless, for those interested in all facets of New England's history and growth the town has a bold character, with much of the flavor of a prosperous nineteenth-century industrial community. It also provides a distinct contrast to the delicate rurality of the Cornish area, a few miles to the north (see "Cornish and Vicinity"—page 80).

Claremont's history began, in common with many New Hampshire towns, with a grant from Governor Benning Wentworth in 1764, who named the settlement after the estate of England's Lord Clive, one of Wentworth's many aristocratic colleagues. At first there was little activity in the area. In fact only three of the original sixty-nine grantees ever settled here, and it was not until the early 1800s that major mills were built, run by waterpower from the Sugar River. At first shoe manufacturing was the town's main industry but, by 1830 a number of woolen mills were flourishing, using the fleece of locally raised Spanish Merino sheep, which had been introduced in 1810 by William Jarvis, the American consul to Spain. By 1846 the vast Monadnock Mills were established, and became the mainstay of Claremont's economy for more than a century.

Mill scene—Claremont

Many of the long, dark mills still stand in Claremont, crammed into the narrow chasm through which the Sugar River churns and tumbles down into the Connecticut. Within the town itself the water drops almost three hundred feet through a series of twisting rapids. According to an early guidebook of the area, every twenty feet of this fall furnished sufficient power for twenty thousand weaving spindles. The noise must have been incredible—the roar of the water, the creaking of the waterwheels, the clatter of machines in the mills. But to the local businessmen it was a beautiful sound, the great cacophony of capital. Many of them built their elaborate mansions within earshot of the mills along wide, tree-lined Broad Street, which was (and remains) a magnificent space, dominated at the northern end by a great brick town hall and a small triangular park complete with bandstand. In the distance, mountains with such strange names as Bible Hill, Flatrock and Twist Back enclose the town and provide a sharp contrast to the extravagant urbanity of the community. Notice the once splendid Hotel Moody in Tremont Square. Old photographs show it a mass of banners and striped awnings over every window, with horse-drawn carriages waiting in line outside the main entrance. Even today, although it has lost much of its former glory, it remains an imposing architectural edifice, complete with odd towers, turrets and chimneys blended in a most unusual asymmetrical form.

A similar description could also apply to another of Claremont's distinctive architectural features—although in the case of the Toy Castle, owner Conrad Lambert is beguilingly modest about his unique creation: "Actually, it was my father's idea. He thought that a toy shop should be fun to look at, and so we started adding all kinds of bits and pieces, and, well, it came out looking like this." "This" refers to a fascinating melange of fort-like towers and battlements, moving figures, fountains, waterfalls, toy trains running past elaborately painted mural scenery and a wishing well—all around, inside or on top of what was originally an old barn. Although this lighthearted creation looks totally out of place in the somber brick and stone mill town, it has attracted an amazing following from all over New England, and there's always some event in progress—a toy fair, the Easter Rabbit Festival, weekly gift giveaways from the wishing well or just the sight of a score of children enthralled by row upon row of toys, games and other playthings.

Another remarkable characteristic of Claremont is the preponderance of churches. This is in part due to the philanthropic attitudes of the town's prominent businessmen, who, in addition to providing a library, a school, a hospital and a bandstand, also supported an opera house, the town band, a symphony orchestra and, by all accounts, many of the churches. A second, equally important factor was the diversity of Claremont's population. This was no unidenominational town. Russian-American residents, who moved here during the prosperous mill period, built their own Russian Orthodox Church, a most unusual feature of the town. Many

"Toy Castle"—Claremont

St. Mary's Church—West Claremont

Polish families, mainly from the Wilno region of Poland, joined to form the Thaddeus Kosciusko Society and ultimately established their own Catholicism-based church, Saint Joseph's. Mormons, Calvary Baptists, Christian Scientists, Nazarenes, Methodists, Jehovah's Witnesses, Lutherans, Seventh Day Adventists and the Temple Meyer-David congregation—all have their own worship centers in the town. Any visitor must be impressed by their architectural variety—but perhaps the most attractive of all is tiny Saint Mary's Church, just off the main road in West Claremont. This unusual brick structure, the first Roman Catholic church in New Hampshire, was built in 1823 by Father Virgil Barber across from elegant Union Church, erected in 1768. Ironically Barber's father was an Episcopalian minister here until he followed his son into the Catholic faith in the mid-1820s.

Although Roman Catholicism in the area lapsed for a few decades, in the 1890s a dynamic Irish priest, Father Patrick J. Finnegan, helped restore the faith and founded Saint Mary's School and Convent in four of the town's finest old homes, on Central Street just off Tremont Square. These structures, with their Classical facades, still exist as ample evidence of the sumptuous style in which Claremont's entrepreneurs once lived.

Clarendon Springs Hotel

13. CLARENDON SPRINGS AND VICINITY
Springs and Spas of the Green Mountains

"Best water in these parts by far." The large lady in a loose flower-patterned dress stooped over a short piece of copper pipe; water gushed out into a half-gallon plastic milk container. "This is the last. You want some? You better get some." Nine other containers stood in a line on a nearby rock. They were all full. "We've been coming here, my family and me, for more than twelve years. People used to pay for this water, you know. That's where they used to drink it." The lady pointed up the hill to a small shingled building with a steep-pitched roof and elaborately carved window frames. "Used to sit there, in their fine dresses and things, and drink it. Used to pay, too." She roared a great laugh. Someone in the battered stationwagon across the stream hit the horn twice. "Used to call this 'baby water.' Families in these parts were big, real big." She looked down at the stationwagon as she loaded a fold-up cart with her containers. "We done pretty good, too—them's all mine, you know." She pointed to the array of arms, knees, legs and peering faces that seemed to fill every corner of the wagon. "Eleven and still going strong." She smacked her belly with her fist and set off down the hill, and then she paused. "You married?" I smiled and nodded. "Get yourself some of that water, then!" She roared another great laugh and waved as the heavy cart pulled her down the hill.

Baby water? Actually the legend seems to have some merit. A census taken in the late 1800s showed that the eight families within the vicinity of Clarendon Springs had produced a grand total of 113 children, most of whom attended the same school. Little wonder that the small community attracted such an enthusiastic trade during the early nineteenth century. This was the era of the spa—a time when the royal and the rich of Europe spent languorous weeks every year at fashionable resorts drinking strange-flavored spring water (the stranger the better) and telling each other how much better they felt. Baden-Baden, Bath, Harrogate, Tunbridge Wells, Castlemaine—these were some of the great spas of Europe, although a host of smaller towns gained instantaneous and equal recognition as expert chemists found more and more medicinal springs in the valleys and mountains of Germany, France, England and Ireland.

Americans, particularly following the Revolution, decided to find their own springs and start their own spas, impelled by the then prevalent "anything Europe can do . . ." spirit. Not very surprisingly, medicinal waters were found in abundance. Western New England was a particularly popular locale, and resorts were developed at Sheldon, Alburg Springs, Tunbridge, Plainfield, Brunswick, Williamstown, Vergennes. However, the classic resort was Clarendon. Not only were its waters supposedly conducive to rampant fertility but, according to a strange mystic, Aza Smith, who discovered the spring in 1776, they also provided a fine remedy for rheumatism, arthritis and "scrofula." While the resort never gained the stature of such later spas as Saratoga, it nevertheless boasted a fine hotel, which still stands today, and a devoted following of Southerners who journeyed north each summer to partake of the waters at the springhouse.

Inevitably the Civil War brought an end to this annual migration, and Clarendon experienced a decline from which it never recovered. Subsequent attempts to revive the spa were unsuccessful, and today the large hotel slowly crumbles on its formerly magnificent grounds. The springhouse remains intact, though, and a peek through one of the holes in the door will reveal the old iron railing surrounding the source of Clarendon's once considerable popularity. For some, of course, such as the large lady with the even larger family, Clarendon is still very much alive!

The source—Clarendon Springs

A few miles to the southwest, along delightful back roads, is a second spa town, Middletown Springs, that seems to have maintained its association with the past a little more successfully than Clarendon Springs. In fact the historical society here recently financed the reconstruction of the springhouse on its original site. It's a delicate little structure set in a

Springhouse—Middletown Springs

small streamside park. There are no fancy signs on the main street showing the way; if you're curious, you'll find it.

Early records indicate the discovery of a medicinal spring here in the late 1700s, but it was apparently lost in the 1811 flood—one of many that have deluged this area in the past two centuries. Then in 1868 a Mr. Gray, inventor and manufacturer of the Gray Horsepower Machine, relocated the spring, and by 1870 Middletown Springs Healing Waters were being not only drunk locally but also bottled and distributed widely throughout New England. As the spa mania gathered momentum the town prospered, and the great Montvert Hotel was opened. Catering to 250 or more guests, it provided an admirable array of genteel recreations: croquet, bowls, tennis, string orchestras in the evening. Ladies in their hoopskirts strolled the grounds, parasols a-dither, or walked slowly through the woods to the springhouse for their daily intake of the waters. Again, as with many of the early spa towns, the fortunes of Middletown Springs declined. By 1927 the source had been lost again under the silt of another flood, and a few years later the hotel burned down. However, the enthusiasm of today's local residents that led to the restoration of the springhouse is likely to revive interest in this charming little hill town, although by the looks of the local cider mill, tourism will never be taken too seriously in these parts!

The same can hardly be said for the nearby village of East Poultney, whose residents appear to take very seriously indeed their historical links with Horace Greeley—almost to the point where one wonders if the town should not be renamed Greeleyville in honor of that remarkable founder of the New York *Tribune*. However, it's doubtful that Horace, if he were alive, would countenance such an idea. He was hardly known for his sentimentality.

Just off the green, a fine triangular space dominated by the early-nineteenth-century Baptist church, is the old Eagle Tavern. Now a private house, the building with its oddly spaced columns is an interesting example of Southern-influenced Colonial architecture. Greeley lived here briefly while working as a typesetter in the local newspaper office at Poultney along with George Jones, later one of the founders of the New York *Times*. A smaller house facing the green also became a Greeley home for a couple of years, and the schoolhouse bears a plaque commemorating Horace's first political speech at the age of fourteen.

The great editor's early publishing ventures were not particularly successful, but the *Tribune,* which he began in 1841, was an appropriate

Cider mill—near Middletown Springs

vehicle for this adamant social reformer, supporter of universal suffrage and political aspirant. In 1848 he became a member of Congress, and worked for a further quarter century to bring about liberal changes in American democracy. East Poultney is a living memorial to one of the nation's most interesting if controversial characters.

Farther to the east, past the spring towns, are a number of delightful country roads crisscrossing the rolling Green Mountains around Wallingford. To the north is the sparse little community of Plymouth, birthplace and longtime home of Calvin Coolidge, who was perhaps the most "Vermont" of all famous Vermonters. A little farther south, the village of Mount Holly slumbers above a deep wooded valley. Some of its homes, including a superbly detailed mansion, have apparently been abandoned. Yet this same area was the scene of frantic activity over a century ago when the Rutland and Vermont Central Railroad Companies raced to provide the first train service from Boston to Burlington. The Rutland Railroad Company finally won; and on December 18, 1849, an elaborate victory celebration, complete with eloquent speeches, cannon salutes, toasts and a "mingling of the waters" ceremony was held at the summit of the pass in the midst of a swirling snowstorm!

It's hard to believe that this pastoral region of rolling hills, winding back roads and quiet streams was once such a lively area. Today many of the railroad tracks are silent and weed-grown; the great spa hotels are gone. Maybe it's the large ladies with plastic milk containers who keep the area thriving. After all, the baby water still runs free!

East Poultney

14. CORNISH AND VICINITY
Artists, Writers and "Lincoln-Shaped Men"

The history of the Connecticut Valley around Windsor and the Cornish villages reads like a *Who's Who* of the art and literary world of the late 1800s. The rolling, wooded hills on the east side of the valley became, for almost half a century, the "Beverly Hills" of New England—a cultural enclave of the brilliant minds and talents of the day. The word "colony" is often used to describe the group that settled here, but, in a similar way to the MacDowell Colony to the south near Peterborough (a secluded estate of studios where Thornton Wilder, Aaron Copland, Roy Harris and scores of others found inspiration), the Cornish group was loosely knit and eludes cultural classification. Most of the resident artists and writers had distinctive, often contrasting reputations and tastes, as evidenced by the variety in size and style of the homes—most of which are totally invisible from the main roads in the area.

Maxfield Parrish lived just outside Plainfield in a large mansion set in an estate of gigantic oaks. Once known simply as "The Oaks," the mansion is now a fine restaurant and inn, Wells Wood. Winston Churchill, whose political novel *Coniston* is set in the Cornish area, also lived close by. President Woodrow Wilson was so enamored of the writer's estate, Harlakenden, that he leased the property for the first three years of his administration as a summer White House.

Residence of Augustus Saint-Gaudens—near Plainfield

Although in its heyday the region became home for a score of well-known writers and artists, the most prominent resident at the turn of the century was without doubt the sculptor Augustus Saint-Gaudens, creator of the famous standing "Lincoln" statue, now in Chicago. Saint-Gaudens, born in Dublin, Ireland, in 1848, was brought at the age of six months to New York by his French father and Irish mother. Due to the family's poverty his formal education was cut short, but he later managed to study at the Cooper Union in Manhattan and eventually saved enough money to work at the Ecole des Beaux-Arts in Paris. During a visit to Rome he gained a wealthy American patron, and in 1876 was awarded his first public commission, for the Farragut Monument in Madison Square, New York.

Saint-Gaudens visited the Cornish area during his creative prime in 1885, following the standing "Lincoln" commission. His friends persuaded him that Cornish and vicinity were filled with "plenty of Lincoln-shaped men," and eventually he settled here for the last seven years of his life in an old brick tavern known locally as "Huggins' Folly." The sculptor was not too happy with the tavern's appearance, which he likened to "an austere, upright, New England farmer with a new set of false teeth." So he undertook a major remodeling of the building, and also transformed the landscape of his hilltop estate, creating lawns, opening up broad vistas of the Connecticut Valley and magnificent Mount Ascutney, planting new groves of trees and building studios, the most impressive of which was the Studio of the Pergola. It was here, beneath the north-facing window, that Saint-Gaudens produced some of his

"Plain" church—near South Cornish

most important work. Even a disastrous fire that destroyed one of his "Lincoln" statues, a series of bas-reliefs, years of sketches and notes and all his correspondence with his friend Robert Louis Stevenson, did not deter him; he continued to work vigorously on his many projects until his death in 1907.

Today the house and grounds, including studios, lawns and a fine collection of Saint-Gaudens' works, are authentically preserved up the steep hill off the main valley road near Plainfield, the only recent addition being a couple of studio cottages available to artists. The setting is almost too idyllic. I remember a warm summer afternoon, lying on the grass by the main studio and listening to a chamber orchestra, made up mainly of local musicians, playing a Mozart concerto as the breeze rustled leaves and bees buzzed in the flowers. There were perhaps a hundred or so other people there, some sitting in picnic groups surrounded by wicker baskets, all totally enraptured by the atmosphere. It is a perfect setting for the sculptor's great romantic works—"Victory" (a replica of the Central Park monument) the powerful statue "The Puritan," studies for the standing "Lincoln," the austere Adams Memorial and the pre-Raphaelite Farragut Monument.

Somehow this whole Cornish region has an almost magical quality to it. It's a beautiful landscape of deep woods, rolling hills, glimpses of streams and the river and of great mansions hidden down narrow lanes. Everywhere there are mysterious back roads, some leading nowhere, others passing through the small Cornish communities with their tiny churches. This church, set alone in a field near South Cornish, is one of my favorites, possibly because of its total lack of embellishment. It was founded in 1793 by Philander Chase of Corinth, who became the first Episcopal bishop of Ohio (1819) and later of Illinois. The nearby Saint Mary's Church at West Claremont (see "Claremont"—page 73) bears a striking resemblance to this simple building.

The area is also rich in covered bridges, the most impressive being the 468-foot-long Cornish Bridge across the Connecticut at Windsor, which at one point in its checkered history was completely demolished and swept downstream by a huge ice jam in the river. The nearby community of Cornish Mills possesses two covered bridges, although much more modest in size and both in urgent need of repair. The most perfect, however, in setting and design is this bridge across Blood Brook, just outside Meriden. Beyond here to the west are also some of the region's best back roads, meandering through the rolling hills into the Connecticut Valley.

Meriden itself is an interesting community. Half of the town nestles in a narrow valley and the rest is located up the hill around Kimball Union Academy, where pleasant brick and frame buildings surround a tree-shaded green. The academy was founded in 1813 as a training school for ministers, and subsequently broadened its charter to serve as a preparatory school for Dartmouth College.

But Meriden's true reputation, and its nickname of the "Bird Village," stems from the activities of Ernest Harold Baynes in the area. He was an enthusiastic naturalist who arrived in 1910 to study the habits of wild animals in the Blue Mountain Forest Reservation in Sullivan County. This 24,000-acre private park, once owned by railroad entrepreneur Austin Corbin, contained a wide range of North American animals, including a

Covered bridge—Meriden

Birdbath in Meriden Bird Sanctuary

large herd of purebred buffalo. Baynes continually emphasized the need to protect natural wildlife, and his book *Wild Bird Guests—How to Entertain Them* led to the establishment of the Meriden Bird Club, which rapidly became a model for a nationwide network of bird protection societies. Within a short time Meriden bird lovers created a unique protective reserve for local birds, on wooded farmland just beyond the academy, featuring a virtual metropolis of elaborately designed birdhouses—some four and five stories high, with columned facades and porticoed entrances.

The Helen Woodruff Smith Sanctuary, as it was called, still exists today. It's a little overgrown and unkempt, but within its thirty or so acres can be found a fascinating array of these birdhouses, although some of the more ornate examples have disappeared. Few people come here, so it's a beautiful place for a quiet afternoon walk. Just follow the main path—and look out for what must be the most elaborate birdbath ever devised. This bronze edifice, set in a leafy dell and covered with delicate bas-reliefs, was sculpted by Mrs. Louis Saint-Gaudens, who was no mean artist herself, in memory of the bird masque *Sanctuary* performed here in 1913. Masques were a popular theatrical form at this time. The twentieth anniversary of Augustus Saint-Gaudens' first visit to Cornish was celebrated by the *Masque of the Golden Bowl* in 1905; and *Sanctuary*'s author, Percy MacKaye, was best known for his masque *St. Louis*—which required 7500 citizens of St. Louis as performers! From all accounts *Sanctuary* was a brilliant event, attended by President Wilson and featuring his daughter Margaret and Ernest Harold Baynes in the cast. Visitors will note that the complete cast is recorded for posterity on the side of the birdbath.

This tiny region indeed has magic. There are few other places in New England possessing such an unusual, yet totally charming, history.

15. CANAAN AND THE NORTHERN LAKES
Lakes, Ponds and Pools

My main recollection of this region is swimming; swimming in lakes, ponds and pools, at dawn, in the afternoon, at dusk and once around two A.M., following a lengthy and convivial conversation with a fellow traveler over two bottles of fine Bordeaux wine. In this northern part of New Hampshire's lake country there are still plenty of places where, without formality of any kind, you can park the car by the roadside and bathe in fresh, clean waters undisturbed by others—alone in a hidden corner all your own.

I particularly remember Webster Lake, just outside Franklin. It's not very secluded (in fact the beach runs alongside the main road), but at six-thirty in the morning there's little chance of being disturbed. I swam through a mirror-smooth surface. The trees lining the lake's edge were reflected perfectly in the water, even to the gold on their leaves where the first shafts of sun flashed in drops of dew. There was no sound at all, just the gentle movement of mist in thin strands over the water. I turned and let myself float, watching the day begin.

To the north is the village of Hebron, alongside Newfound Lake—the "hermit of the New Hampshire lakes." Hebron itself, at least the older part around the green, is an appealing place with one of those long, rambling general stores. But again, my memories are of swimming in the lake at sunset when Mount Tenney, the islands and the water were all cocooned in a pink and purple haze. Apparently the Algonkian Indians must have found this place equally attractive, for excavations have shown that this was the site of many of their camps. Captain John Smith, the English explorer, visited the area in 1735, but must have come on a bad day; all he could find to record in his journal was the fact that "the land is very full of great hills and mountains and very rocky." He should have tried swimming in the lake at sunset!

To the west of Hebron is one of my favorite swimming holes, or rather a series of holes, in an area known as the Sculptured Rocks. There are only a few spasmodic signs indicating the way along bumpy back roads—but just keep going west from the village till you reach this small and lovely place. The turbulent Cockermouth River suddenly plunges thirty feet through a narrow gap, and in its fury has gouged strange, smooth shapes in the rock—potholes many feet deep. During the summer, when the river is low, it's a perfect place for a quiet swim, although even then I was surprised at how deep some of the pools were. There was one in particular where the river moved slowly by a ledge of rock over a black hole. After three long dives I had never found the bottom, and decided to let someone else do the exploring.

One of the most attractive lakes in the region is still farther to the west of Hebron, at Canaan Center above the pleasant village of Canaan. The town beach is situated just by the library, but unfortunately its use is restricted to residents of the community. And what a community! The mile-long main street, reached after a steep climb up the valley road, has the same refined dignity as such other exclusive New England communities as Sharon and Litchfield, both in Connecticut (see "Cornwall and Vicinity"—page 18). Fine white mansions, many of the Colonial style, are set back from the road at regular intervals behind lines of old elm trees. Those on the west of the street look over the mountain ranges of the Connecticut Valley, and most of those on the east back directly on the lake itself. Although there are a few discordant elements (a couple of gaudy summer cottages look strangely out of place), Canaan gives the appearance of having been designed as a complete unit. In fact that's exactly what its founders had in mind—they wanted to create an impressive center for the township of Canaan in a commanding situation befitting the status of many of its early citizens. So in 1788 they bludgeoned a steep track through the dense wilderness to the summit of the hill and carefully laid out the town alongside the lake.

Canaan Center is not the only planned settlement in the region. Farther west, on Lake Mascoma, is a former Shaker colony originally established

A street—Canaan

by two ministers from Vermont, now owned by La Salette Seminary, a Roman Catholic institution. The most impressive remaining structure of the original community is the great four-story hall, constructed of Canaan stone in 1840. At the time of its completion it was, with the exception of the state capitol, the most expensive building in New Hampshire—an indication of the commercial success of Shaker enterprises. In fact this must have been one of the most durable of any of the nineteen Shaker communities scattered around the eastern states, for according to a 1916 guidebook of the area the village was still thriving then; the author notes, "Brooms, woolen goods and seeds are for sale." Alas—no more. Most of the buildings are now in use as part of the seminary, and the steep, wooded hillside behind has been converted into an exact replica of the Notre Dame de la Salette shrine near Grenoble, France. Although beautiful in itself, it looks a little incongruous in such a natural landscape.

A third planned community in the region is Hill, a "new village" on the west side of the Franklin Falls Reservoir north of Franklin. It must have been an interesting creative exercise for the planners and architects who worked on the concept in the 1940s. The original village was submerged by the reservoir, and most of the inhabitants were relocated in this comprehensively refurbished environment, which came complete with quaint, winding streets, Colonial-style homes, church, school, community hall, village green and pond (now a little overgrown).

Perhaps the most fascinating settlements in this part of New Hampshire are those lost in the forest or tucked away in tiny valleys along the bumpy back roads that provide the most interesting way to explore the area. Alexandria is an unspoiled village high on a fertile plateau above Newfound Lake. The views to the north, of Mount Cardigan and Mount Baldface, with its sheer rock incline 1200 feet high, are superb and there's a track from the town that leads into Cardigan State Park. There are some excellent climbs here, particularly up the granite slopes of Baldface. On the north side of the range another mountain road ascends from the Canaan Valley up through the tiny community of Orange, with its little town hall and white church, and into the same state park.

However, my favorite drive in this area is along the rough track beyond Canaan Center past Goose Pond (a fine recreation reservoir) and through the wooded hills to Lyme. Somewhere along the way I found this ornate birdhouse—a masterpiece of folk architecture!

Birdhouse—
near Goose Pond

Lyme, although situated along the main road, has retained much of its stately charm. At the top end of the village, by the old Lyme Inn, is an ornate, domed Congregational church, and facing it at the lower end of the long, tree-lined green is the large Hamilton House, with monitor roof and an elaborate Doric-columned facade. It was built in 1810 by the town's doctor on the site of an earlier house that had burned to the ground during construction. The villagers had ridiculed the doctor for the first structure, which they considered gross in both size and scale. So when it came to reconstruction the proud physician built an even larger residence featuring a strange conglomeration of varied architectural influences.

Finally (though it is really outside the region), no traveler should miss a trip to Orford, situated close to the Connecticut River a few miles north of Lyme. The charm of this place, with its seven white "ridge" mansions, was noted by Washington Irving: "In all my travels in this country and in Europe, I have seen no village more beautiful than this." What further recommendation could be asked?

Goose Pond

The Notch road

16. SANDWICH AND VICINITY
Moses Hall and the Sandwich Notch

One of the first land surveyors of the Sandwich grant, Daniel Beede, described in his official report the wild landscape of this part of New Hampshire's White Mountains: "No where in the prospect ahead is there a piece as big as the palm of my hand that is not covered with forest."

How very true! Of course, as with many of New England's mountainous regions, there was a brief but intense period of lumbering near Sandwich, and even the establishment of small settlements around patches of cleared land. But eventually the forest grew back, covering the lumber-railroad tracks, toppling the stone walls and filling the cellar holes. Today it is just as Mr. Beede described it—a landscape thick with forest, where little sign of man's brief tenure remains.

I first approached Sandwich from the north along the Notch road. It was a fresh, clear White Mountains morning as I drove off Interstate 93 through the onetime artists' resort of Campton and up the Mad River Valley. The road had been recently improved due to the popularity of the Waterville Valley Ski Resort just below Mount Osceola, and the river, an alarmingly furious flood during the spring months, was pleasantly docile.

It's hard to miss the entrance to the Notch road, a gloomy tunnel of dark shadows, approached up a steep incline past warning signs that would make most motorists, if they valued their automobiles, turn back immediately. Fortunately my machine was old, thoroughly tested on rough roads and had a high clearance (although, as I was to find out later, not quite high enough!).

The first part was disarmingly easy. The track rose quickly through the woods onto a meadowland plateau dotted with a few barns and cottages. The view of the great Mad River Mountains—Tecumseh, Whiteface and Tripyramid—was superb. Shadows from puffy clouds moved over the dark green forest on their flanks, and the summits, flecked with outcrops of white rock, gleamed in the bright morning sunshine. I looked forward to the other vistas from the Notch road—little realizing that this would in fact be both the first and the last.

For the next few miles the track followed every undulation of the terrain. There had been no attempts (and hopefully there never will be) to smooth the surface, remove the hairpin turns, reduce the ridiculous grade, or make the track wide enough for two vehicles to pass without playing "chicken"—although there was once a gentleman who tried to keep the Notch road at least negotiable. His name was Moses Hall. He lived, along with a few other hardy settlers, on the south side of the Notch, a few miles north of Center Sandwich. Not too much is known about him, except that he became the self-appointed guardian of the road during the early 1900s, at a time when it was still one of the main trade routes between the northwestern hinterland and Portsmouth. Hall's home was always open to the needy traveler. When he wasn't clearing land for local farmers he would be somewhere along the track, filling in holes, removing obstacles or "breaking" snowdrifts that in some years lay as deep as twenty feet—even in the middle of June. When he died he left his accumulated savings to the township, with instructions that they be used to keep local roads in good repair.

Apparently not much has been spent on the Notch road. It was just after I passed the highest point (a little hand-lettered sign nailed to a tree recorded the elevation as 1776 feet) that I lost part of my exhaust system crashing through a puddle that turned out to be more like a pond. My poor vehicle began to creak and rumble, and it was with some relief that I saw another hand-painted sign, this one for Beede Falls.

I parked and strolled through shadow-dimpled woods, into what has become for me one of the most beautiful little corners of New England. The main waterfall that scampers down a great slab of smooth white rock is only the beginning of a long series of cascades and pools. In some places the stream lies deep and still, the water clear yet brown, like the earth, against the light-colored boulders. Little green pads of moss grow

Center Sandwich

where water oozes from the rock like yolk from a cracked eggshell. Orange and bronze toadstools resembling tiny balls of dough emerge in clusters from rotting limbs of trees. A small green leaf still full of summer juices revolves round and round in a whirling pool—a drop of water on its surface gleams like a cut diamond. The stream bursts from bushes full of soft shadows; lower down it swooshes and chitters over the smooth rock and tumbles, balls of sparkling quicksilver, into darker pools where silt and pebbles have settled for the summer. Overhead the leaves droop in a dark green canopy. Roots crawl in cracks, splitting boulders, holding others like great claws or writhing, serpent-like, across rocks before plunging deep into the mossy earth.

I have written many lines and thought many thoughts here. It's a very precious place. Those who visit seem to treat it with the love and respect it deserves. It could so easily be spoiled—it needs only one transistor radio or a few abandoned soda cans.

As the Notch road approaches Center Sandwich it improves dramatically. In fact at this point it's such an attractive-looking route that many motorists approaching the Notch from the southern end decide to ignore all the warnings, and gaily set off on what invariably turns out to be a most nerve-wracking fifteen-mile safari.

At first Center Sandwich seems to consist primarily of handicrafts workshops and outlets. Actually the impression is accurate, for it was here that the Sandwich Home Industries started in 1926, and later led to the formation of a statewide movement—the New Hampshire League of Arts and Crafts—that has helped preserve many of New England's traditional domestic crafts. Even the disastrous fire of 1934, which destroyed many of the old buildings in the central part of the village, in no way discouraged progress. A new industry center was erected and most of the handicrafts outlets were reopened. Today Center Sandwich is a thriving community, with a fine historical society exhibit near the town hall and a reputation all over New England for its Old Home Week, usually held in late August, and its annual fair on October 12.

The town has been quite used to popularity ever since the 1890s, when nearby Squam Lake became a fashionable resort area with steamers, ferries, lakeside cottages and a beach. The 1891 Sandwich directory lists two hotels and eighteen boardinghouses, with weekly rates varying between $5 and $12. Fortunately much of the summer furor of the late nineteenth century has now gone; Center Sandwich entertains a more discriminating clientele of artists, whose favorite subject seems to be the local Baptist church, as well as history lovers who find much of interest in the historical society's excellent museum. With the exception of the annual fair day and Old Home Week the village retains its quiet character for most of the year.

The road to the south passes through the village of Sandwich, originally known as Lower Corner. This was once the most populous community in the Sandwich grant, but little remains except two fine old mansions and

Durgin Bridge—North Sandwich

an unusual red brick store. In contrast the nearby town of Moultonborough, situated on the northern tip of New Hampshire's famous resort lake Winnipesaukee, is a thriving place, with an "old country store" that attracts a continuous throng of tourists all summer long. Few visitors, however, notice the unusual feature just across the road—a virtual village of birdboxes along the side of a large wooden shed.

The road east from Center Sandwich leads to the scattered community of North Sandwich and passes Durgin Bridge, the only covered bridge in the area. Continuing eastward through Whiteface and Tamworth, the narrow lane passes many miles of fine woodland scenery before entering the bustling town of Conway. It was in this area of the Ellis River Valley, centered at North Conway, that the famous White Mountain School of artists flourished in the late 1800s, drawing inspiration from the awesome scenery of Mount Washington and the Presidential Range.

From Conway there's a magnificent drive westward along the Kancamagus Highway to Interstate 93 at Lincoln. This route is one of the most scenic in New England, and I suggest you allow at least half a day to stop at all the gorges and waterfalls and possibly to visit the superbly designed Loon Lodge and Resort at the western end, just outside Lincoln. It's a great way to complete an exploration of this southern part of the White Mountains.

17. BRISTOL AND THE LINCOLN GAP
Fall in the Green Mountains

It was a perfect fall morning. A thick layer of mist lay in the little valleys as I drove northward from Middlebury to Bristol. Above the mist it was sparkling clear; the western ridges of the Green Mountains, flecked with silver where frost still clung to the trees, were clearly outlined against an already deep blue sky. There were no clouds and the sun was without a haze—a bright white ball in a landscape of bronzed foliage.

Bristol is a pleasant town, located on a broad terrace halfway up the long climb into the mountains. Its spacious green boasts a fine bandstand—although the recent demise of the Bristol Inn and its replacement by an innocuous supermarket has destroyed much of the architectural harmony of this space. Even the clean white buildings on the north side and the unusually ornate brick town hall on the south cannot disguise the unfortunate gap, now filled with cars, at the top end of the green.

Bristol's charm is mainly to be found in its history—particularly in the legend of buried treasure said to be located a couple of miles south of town, somewhere on a rocky hillside known as Hell's Half Acre. Of course, as those familiar with New England folktales will know, this is only one of many treasures supposedly hidden in fields and forests from Long Island to the Canadian border. Vermont seems to have been an especially popular hiding place, and over the years as many as twenty-five locations, including sites around Essex, Brandon, Ludlow, Wells and Braintree, have attracted devoted pick-and-shovel-wielding fortune hunters. At least four sites in the state are reputedly the resting place of Captain Kidd's ill-gotten gains (and three other sites throughout New England also claim the honor, including an island in the Connecticut River near Northfield, Massachusetts). However, as far as is known no treasure has ever been found in Hell's Half Acre, and the scores of individuals who have hacked, blasted and bored away here have invariably left disillusioned, frustrated and bankrupt. Yet until recent times, when there have been moves to include the site in a federal wilderness area, an occasional optimist would still scale the steep hillside through thick forest to chip away among the rocks of this mysterious place where, according to a local historian, "all is gloom and solitude, gloomy caverns . . . in the innermost recesses of the ledges; the hollow rumbling of subterranean cataracts . . . the solemn roar of the wind in the mountain pine . . . all help to prepare the mind to take in the wild legends that hover over this spot."

And the legends certainly abound. There's the one about the wizened Spaniard who first came to find his father's buried cache of silver; tales of ghosts and evil spirits guarding the treasure—and even the story of Simeon Coreser, who established a lucrative company to finance his search for the treasure and who directed diggings based on consultations with his private occultist. According to a local ballad, the "Ballad of Old Pocock" (a previous name for Bristol), his partners actually found the

Roadside cascade—near Bristol

treasure but Coreser, through a series of devious tricks, managed to steal it from right under their noses. However, there are many who think the treasure still lies in Hell's Half Acre, perhaps buried under an old landslide. But if the wilderness area proposal is accepted, it's unlikely that digging will ever be resumed.

The road climbs steeply out of Bristol, past this beautiful cascade, and up onto a high plateau. Here a choice of direction has to be made. From the community of Lincoln there's a long trail south through the mountains that ends at Ripton, onetime home of the "poet laureate of Vermont," Robert Frost. A few miles farther down the road from Ripton is Bread Loaf, an unusual settlement where the Bread Loaf School of English is organized annually by Middlebury College. This course in the appreciation and creation of literature has been in existence since 1920 and attracts students from all parts of the country.

An alternate journey across the mountains is the one over Route 17, which swings to the north away from the Lincoln Gap road after the first long climb out of Bristol. The initial part of the drive is across a narrow valley of cornfields; then the road ascends again through forest to the community of Jerusalem. Here the dense mixture of pines and maples gives way to open, rolling fields and splendid vistas of the mountains to the north—particularly the proud profile of Mount Ethan Allen with its scarred rockface.

The final climb up through the Appalachian Gap is the most impressive. The road twists and turns with almost alpine dexterity to a high point of 2356 feet. No one should fail to park in the small area provided at the summit. The view westward toward the Champlain ranges is one of the most striking in a region renowned for its dramatic scenery. The long descent to Waitsfield and the Mud River Valley seems almost anticlimactic by comparison.

A third alternative route through the mountains is one of my favorites. It leaves Route 17 a few miles north of Jerusalem and continues northward, partway on unsurfaced track, through the Huntingdons to the

Cemetery—Huntingdon Center

Winooski River Valley, east of Burlington. There are no alarming climbs and dramatic vistas along here. Rather it is as if one had returned to a Vermont of yesteryear—an unspoiled enclave reflecting the steady pace of rural life in the Green Mountains. Admittedly some unwelcome and obvious reminders of twentieth-century life have changed the northern end near Burlington, but for the most part this is a fine drive through an open valley. The small villages reflect a spartan existence; many of the homes badly need a coat of paint, and the churches lack much of the elaborate ornamentation of their lowland counterparts. The cemeteries, such as the one here at Huntingdon Center, tell numerous sad tales of early death and deep sorrow. Yet the simple beauty of the valley, a bowl of scarlets and bronzes during the fall, somehow relieves what would be in other settings an air of oppressive poverty.

It was in areas like this that the Yankee spirit was molded and strengthened. Huntingdon's James Johns is a good example. During the more than sixty-three years that he lived here in the village he hand-printed a remarkable series of stories, poems, musical compositions, diaries, weather journals and, best known of all, his *Vermont Autograph and Remarker*. This tiny four-page, double-column newspaper—approximately five by three inches—was produced regularly until a few weeks before his death in 1874. As can be seen from the Johns collection in the Vermont Historical Society Museum in Montpelier, his penmanship was of such high standard that it's often difficult to distinguish it from metal typeface.

Johns was a meticulous recordkeeper. No local event escaped his notice, and most, no matter how apparently trivial, were committed to paper. If the event seemed particularly significant to him he would compose a musical ditty:

> There was an old chap in the west country,
> A flaw in his lease the lawyers had found.
> 'Twas all about felling five oak trees
> And building a house upon his own ground.
> Ritoo dinoo, ritoo dinoo, ritoo dinoo dinaa!

However, it is his *Vermont Autograph* that best illustrates his editorial ability, his love of rhetoric:

> The people are heartily sick of violated pledges, broken promises and false confessions of democracy most outrageously belied in the anti-republican, monarchist disposition manifested by the late and present executive, and are desirous of change in the mode of administration to purge the depths of the odious corruption both practiced and tolerated.
>
> September 10th, 1840

Somehow the sentiments of this indomitable Yankee appear very familiar even today!

The fourth, and last alternative, route across the Green Mountains east of Bristol is through the Lincoln Gap. This relatively short, ten-mile drive from the village of Lincoln is one of the most dramatic and exciting experiences in Vermont. It requires a sturdy vehicle and even sturdier nerves, but the rewards are many, particularly if the pace is leisurely and the weather clear. When you reach the summit—a mighty 2424 feet—it's worth leaving the car and briefly following the Long Trail in either direction to gaze on the panoramas that unfold, most notably of the mountain ranges along Lake Champlain to the west. The beauty of these mountains, particularly in fall, sets me in a kind of emotional limbo that can last for hours and seems unaffected even by the adrenalin-churning descent into the Mud River Valley.

Warren, the quiet community at the end of the Gap road with its covered bridge, is always a welcome sight. If you or the car have had enough rough riding for the day, Warren is a good place to end the journey. However, if you can manage one more cross-mountain jaunt, try the Warren–Roxbury road. This is somewhat shorter and less tortuous than the Lincoln Gap road, but the views of the Mud River Valley make it well worthwhile. I remember parking my car on a hot fall day high up on the hillside and sitting for what must have been a couple of hours watching gliders spiraling above the valley and around the mountaintops, as the currents carried them higher and higher into a cloudless sky. The silence made my ears ring.

Covered bridge—Warren

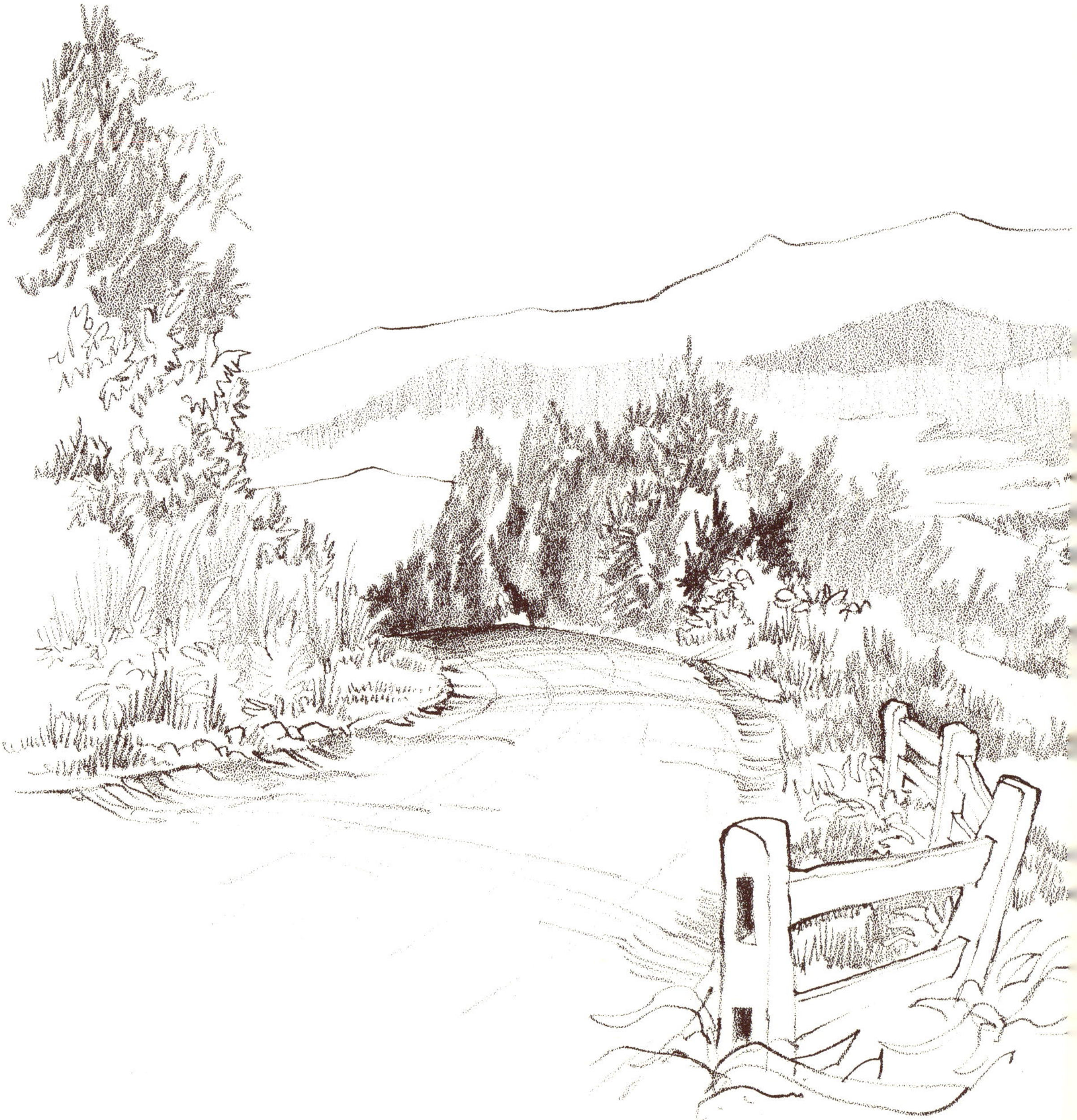

Green Mountains panorama—near Warren

18. THE MONTPELIER LAKE COUNTRY
Some Notable Vermont Characters

Just a few short miles north of Montpelier and its twin city, Barre (the "Granite Capital of America"), is a beautiful, unspoiled landscape dotted with tiny ponds and lakes. I spent many days roaming its back lanes, chatting with the villagers, sitting quietly by the side of streams or swimming in its forest-enclosed waters. There's a special kind of tranquility here. The villages are true Vermont: not so much the pristine white settlements of southern New England but rather "lived-in" places, a little battered, a little gnarled by the rigors of the climate and the strenuous rural life. Signs of poverty are not uncommon. Nothing has been done to disguise the fact that this is a hard-working corner of the state.

Yet beauty is everywhere. This view is typical of vistas seen from the hills around Calais and Woodbury. Farther to the west, among the lakes and forests, the scenery is more enclosed, more intimate. I spent an autumn day by a small lake near North Calais (I believe its local name is Cranberry Meadow Pond), and not one car passed on the track, nothing disturbed the silence. Hawks and eagles would occasionally circle above the forest and then, carried by currents, drift beyond the skyline in search of an afternoon snack. There were fish in the pond; sometimes one would jump clean out of the water in a flash of silver and then disappear in a flurry of splashes and ripples. Squirrels hunted for acorns along the tiny beach by the side of the track. One, a strange little creature with part of an ear missing, sat almost within arm's reach, waiting to join me in my sandwich lunch. Unfortunately he didn't like salami.

Traveling this relatively small corner, I became aware of the number of notable characters the region seems to have produced. I'm not referring to men of great political or financial stature but rather to individuals who gained fame in unusual ways—often quite reluctantly. For example, to the west near Burlington is the small village of Jericho, once the home of W. A. Bentley, the "Snowflake Man." Quietly and systematically, over many years, Bentley made more than five thousand photographic portraits of individual snowflakes. He never discussed his work with anyone until, by chance, he was "discovered" working in conditions of extreme poverty by Reverend Henry Crocker of Fairfield, Vermont. The reverend wrote an article for a learned journal on Bentley's studies, and within a short time the shy photographer had gained worldwide recognition. However, although he benefited financially from all the attention, Bentley continually bemoaned the fact that public appearances and lectures played havoc with his regular photographic schedule.

The tiny village of Cabot, on the eastern fringe of this lakeland region, was once known for its twelve whiskey distilleries, a considerable number for such a small place (although nearby Peacham once boasted forty-two). More recently the village gained fame as the home of Zerah Colburn, the boy mathematical genius. His skills were such that at the age of nine he was making European tours as a major theatrical attrac-

Typical back road scene—near Calais

tion, and seemed to have a life of luxury and adulation before him. But as he grew older his powers declined, and he died at the age of thirty-four, a forgotten and embittered man.

Calais, a pleasant little community settled around a rather overgrown village pond, was also the home of a number of unusual individuals. Pardon Janes was another child prodigy, famed for his exceptional intelligence and eloquence. His early life was full of achievements and promise, but something went awry as he aged. He developed a permanent aversion to physical human contact of any kind. He even went so far as to wear a pail around his neck to receive purchases from the local store. He invented a remarkable series of instruments to avoid contact with objects touched by human flesh—a purse on the end of a pitchfork for shopping, a special page turner for books, a handle holder for domestic equipment.

Wareham Chase was another Calais resident, a recluse who, without benefit of technical advice or formal learning, developed one of the first electrical motors. Although the Davenport/Smalley engine is recognized as the original version, Chase's remarkable device was considered by many to be far superior in both simplicity of construction and efficiency. It used to be on display at the Vermont Historical Society Museum at Montpelier, but, according to the curator with whom I spoke, it unfortunately seems to have been misplaced.

Another aspect of Calais history is the "freezing story." Somehow it became a popular rumor during the early part of this century that in this village, and other parts of New England where food was scarce in winter, the older, less productive members of the family were "jugged" on whiskey and laid out in the snow to "freeze over." They were then placed in pine boxes that were left in the woods, covered with evergreens, until the spring corn planting. At that time they were thawed out in a bath of cold water, given a good rubdown and another glass of whiskey and welcomed back into the family. This legendary tale of Yankee thrift created so much attention a few years ago that formal denials had to be issued by prominent public officials in the area.

The back roads in the lake country are outstanding. There's a particularly beautiful climb up a rough lane from East Calais to North Calais through dense forest where, on a bright day, the sun filters through the leaves and mottled shadows fill the glades and hollows at the side of the road. In the other direction, from the ramshackle community of Woodbury to Lower Cabot, there's a steep mountain road with panoramic views from the high points. It was along here, just as the road began the long descent into the Winooski River Valley, that I met the Irishman. He lived in a small cottage with a porch full of plants, rocking chairs and wind chimes. I just happened to wave at this old gentleman as I was passing and he signaled me to stop. I did, and he came tripping down the path like a little leprechaun, a wide smile on his face and the blarney twinkle in his eye. We chatted for a few minutes, and then he began a rambling monologue full of humor and folk wisdom. He told me about his family, his sons, life in the mountains, his few acres of ground on which he grew vegetables, the region's history (particularly its once notorious distilleries, which produced the finest potato whiskey in the "Northeast Kingdom" of Vermont), his neighbors and their antics, and finally described in detail his last trip home to County Killarney.

Chandelier, town hall
—Gospel Hollow

The little man poured out his stories, and doubtless he would have enthralled me for hours—but in the middle of a somewhat lurid account of local courting habits he suddenly stopped and listened very intently. In the distance, back up the track, we both heard the rumbling and rattling of an approaching car. "Oh, b'Jese, it's the wife . . . got to go now . . . come again . . . come again, now. . . ." He scuttled up the path and into the house just as an aged Volkswagen trundled around the corner. Its occupant was a rather stern-looking lady. I waved, but she didn't return the acknowledgment. In fact she glanced at me in rather a strong manner and looked around for her errant spouse, who was doubtless watching the whole sequence from behind one of the curtains in the front room. I have an aversion to domestic upsets, and so left somewhat hastily!

There's another fine country drive along the back roads—from Montpelier northward to the crossroads of Maple Corner. Here there are three choices of direction: the route to the west joins Route 12 at Worcester; the route directly ahead wanders north past lakes and ponds to Woodbury, and the eastern route leads to a fascinating museum at Kents' Corner, a mile or so down the road. This Georgian-styled brick building (1837), once a tavern, is now owned by the Vermont Historical Society and is open during the summer (July 4 to September 1, one to five P.M.; closed Mondays). In addition to the individual rooms of the tavern, authentically restored in nineteenth-century style, there's an old-fashioned general store filled with sacks of flour, barrels of apples, old boxes, bottles and notions and potions of every description, plus a more familiar array of souvenirs for the traveler. Just down the hill from the tavern is an old town hall at Gospel Hollow, a tiny place not shown on most maps, where I found this remarkably elaborate chandelier. I was lucky to get inside to make the sketch—it just so happened that the building was being repainted, its first white coat in more than twenty years. The young man busily at work on the steps looked a little disgruntled. Apparently the local people had taken advantage of his generous nature and his skill as a house painter and had persuaded him to take on the mammoth task of repainting, single-handed. He was almost finished—and had just been informed that the village coffers were virtually empty, and that he might have to "wait a while" for remuneration! Nevertheless we spent a delightful half hour chatting about the area, and it was he who directed me to the Old West Church, a mile or so south on the track from the Kent Tavern museum.

There are few structures remaining in New England that reflect as well as this 1824 building the strict, spartan nature of life here around that time. Note the high pews and the lack of ornamentation—no statues, no

Museum and store—Kents' Corner

Old West Church—near Kents' Corner

stained glass, no elaborate carvings. Even the heating system, consisting of two ancient cast iron stoves with a tangle of long pipes suspended from the ceiling, seems to have been added very much as an afterthought. It was doubtless heartily opposed for years by the older, more stoical villagers, who considered frozen feet and fingers to be part of the joy of winter worship!

Although much of Old West Church's history is uneventful, there was an unusual occurrence here on the evening of December 31, 1843. The evangelist William Miller, fanatical leader of a religious sect known as the Millerites, brought his followers to this church to witness the end of the world, which, according to his calculations, would occur precisely in the last minute of the last day of that year. The first stroke of midnight brought a fearful commotion—men turned "ghastly pale and trembled," women screamed and fainted, Mr. Miller waited to be lifted heavenward—but nothing happened. There was no Armageddon; the graves failed to release their dead; Mr. Miller remained where he was, and the congregation finally shuffled out into the cold night wondering what all the fuss had been about.

A final beautiful country drive in this area is along the track past the Old West Church across Route 14 and up the hill on the east side of the valley. Travelers will find themselves on a high ridge that offers a series of wide views of the mountains to the west. Just before the long drop down into East Calais (take the last bend slowly, or you are likely to end up in the church) is one of the few remaining examples in this area of a round barn. These remarkable structures are fast disappearing due to their inordinate cost of maintenance, although there is an even more impressive example near Irasburg to the north (see "The Craftsburys"—page 109).

Round barn—near East Calais

Craftsbury Common

19. THE CRAFTSBURYS
A Tangle of Back Roads

"These kids really get into the land, y'know, I mean, a coupla weeks out of the city and they change—change real fast—you can see it in their faces. They even think differently—they act differently to one another. They seem to care more, y'know—just look at their faces. . . ."

I was chatting on a bright August morning with one of the instructors at the Grassroots Project in Vermont, an educational program of the Sterling Institute, located in a group of white buildings just off the green in Craftsbury Common. And he was right. The kids' faces were tanned and glowing, their eyes sparkling, their walk bounding. Most of them were liberal arts students who had undertaken the thirty-week course in agriculture, forestry and wildlife as a way of broadening their knowledge and appreciation of nature. Some were intending to use their learning directly in the fields of conservation, agriculture and wildlife management; as for the others—well, the course gives credits, it's a great way to spend a year and there's plenty to learn.

And what a place to learn. Craftsbury Common is a crisp little village with a spacious rectangular green, set on top of a steep hill. With the exception of the elaborately detailed Craftsbury Academy, built in 1829, most of the other structures—the church, the Sterling Institute, the homes—possess that restrained quality of early New England architecture and reflect the stern Calvinist characteristics of the township's early Scottish settlers.

For most of the year, except during the peak of the fall color season and around the time of the Banjo and Old-Time Fiddlers Contest in late July, Craftsbury Common is a quiet, pastoral community. I first visited here on an April evening when the chill was still in the air and the dark branches of the trees around the green and down the hill past the inn were just beginning to take on the glow of budding leaves. Using the village as my center point, I set off to explore the mile upon mile of back roads that form a confusing latticework over the rolling hills and dales of Orleans County. This is one of those areas where you need a reliable map. Mine was obviously inadequate, as I ended up sequentially in a farmyard, a swamp and on an impossibly muddy mountain road down which my camper literally slid for at least half a mile, almost missing the tiny bridge at the bottom—which would have put me nose down in a rather ferocious-looking little stream.

In the end I discarded the map and used the sun and my common sense to explore these delightful country lanes. I found tiny lakes and ponds often completely by chance, as they were almost always hidden from the road by dense thickets of trees and bushes. To the north I came across a magnificent specimen of a round barn, at Robillard Flats farm just beyond Irasburg—in fact on a clear day you can just see its roof from the side of the general store on the green. Like most travelers in New England, I'm completely fascinated by this unusual architectural idiom. It seems such a radical departure from the usually conservative and often unimaginative barn designs found throughout the six states.

It appears that the Shakers were one of the first groups to develop the concept of a barn centered around a silo, and today one of the finest examples can be found in the Shaker village of Hancock, Massachusetts. First built in 1826 at the staggering cost of $10,000, it has a circumference of 270 feet and stone walls almost four feet thick in places. Following a fire in 1864, it was rebuilt in 1865 and finally restored as part of the "Village Exhibit" in 1968. The Shakers had a knack for redesigning the most familiar objects in a way that brought new meaning to the ethics of simplicity, economy and beauty. They claimed that the round barn was not only a more sturdy structure than the familiar triangular-brace barn, but also enclosed the maximum amount of floor space for the minimum amount of wall construction.

Unfortunately not all imitations were as successful as the Shakers' structures. One weak segment in a round barn could bring down the whole building, and so various modifications of the concept were introduced over the years, such as Orson Fowler's octagonal barns during the 1850s. However, the design never really caught on, and today through-

Round barn—near Irasburg

out New England there are fewer than twenty round barns left in anything like operating condition. Two others may be found on Route 58 (the Irasburg–Lowell road), but none can match the Robillard Flats barn. I asked one of the farmers why this area should boast so many, and he gave me the kind of answer only a New England farmer could give: "Suppose someone 'round here knew how to build 'em."

While on the subject of unusual architectural phenomena, explorers of this hidden corner will invariably travel along Route 14 and pass through the pleasant community of Albany. Just to the south, set back a little from the road, is the Hayden Mansion, a fine example of a Bulfinch-influenced brick house. Compared with the simple white clapboard structures in the village, this Georgian edifice seems strangely out of place. In fact "strange" is the only way to describe the circumstances of the establishment. It was built in 1854 for William Hayden and his family. Apparently Mr. Hayden had been involved in the construction of almost six hundred miles of the Canadian Pacific Railroad. Having made his fortune, he retired to this country mansion with his family and a full retinue of servants.

Life tended to be rather tumultuous. The Haydens were a hot-blooded lot and there was invariably some feud in progress. Eventually things became so strained that the grandmother, a ferocious tyrant by all accounts, placed a curse on the whole family. As a result, so the story goes, many of the Haydens died prematurely or of mysterious causes, and were buried in the local cemetery. At last the remnants of the family abandoned the accursed mansion, and for years the place was unoccupied. It was then that the villagers began to see strange lights and hear peculiar sounds from the ballroom on the third floor. The mansion gained quite a reputation locally, and in fact many of these unusual incidents were verified. Most people stayed well clear of its overgrown grounds. It was said that the ghostly remains of the Hayden family were forever locked in the house in accordance with the grandmother's curse.

However, since the local vicar moved in, there seems to have been no further problem. In fact the last time I passed I saw a gang of workmen making some major renovations of the south wing. I asked a local storekeeper about the place, and she rejected the whole story as a lot of nonsense. A younger man followed me outside, however, and told me quietly, "I seen those lights. There's something not right down there, I know it." So maybe the mystery remains—but please, don't disturb the vicar!

Or maybe there's something about the air in this lovely corner of Vermont that does things to the imagination. There used to be a story, taken seriously by many locals, that Adolf Hitler was somewhere in hiding along the shore of Caspian Lake near Greensboro. The rumor was possibly due in part to the popularity of that fine stretch of water with various celebrities. Alfred Hitchcock spent much time here while making his movie *The Trouble with Harry* at Craftsbury Common. This was also John Gunther's favorite summer place. Greta Garbo loved the cool, placid waters of the lake, and more recently it has become the locale for a virtual colony of writers, intellectuals and educators from the major New England universities. While the village of Greensboro itself is not particularly outstanding, there's a fine beach just up the hill from the local stores.

Just outside Greensboro to the south is a large monument commemorating the construction of the Hazen Military Road from Peacham to Westfield in 1779. There's a second such monument, to the northwest in the hills beyond Lowell at Hazen's Notch, marking the termination point of this never completed road. It's an interesting if confusing story that indicates the remarkable ambitions of George Washington and his rebels during the early years of the Revolution.

It all began after the disastrous campaign of 1775–76 in which Benedict Arnold and Richard Montgomery tried vainly to conquer Canada. General Bayley convinced General Washington that the key to success of any similar campaign was a fast route into lower Canada. He mapped out such a route beginning at the village of Peacham and crossing fifty-four miles of mostly high ground to the border. On April 29, 1776, Washington gave the go-ahead but cautioned, "I will provide for the expense, which you will be careful in making as light as possible."

General Bayley was sent a $250 advance, and enthusiastically set about building the first six miles of his road—only to receive another letter from Washington a few months later that gloomily forecasted the imminent defeat of the Continental Army in Canada: "There be the strongest reason

Back road scene—near Greensboro

to believe that [our army] will be obliged to abandon possession of that country." So the road was also abandoned—and poor General Bayley was never reimbursed by Congress for his personal financial contribution of almost $750 to the venture.

In 1778, however, the project was revived, and this time General Moses Hazen and his men hacked a trail to the top of the first Green Mountain ridges. But, for various reasons, that's about as far as they got—still forty miles from the target. The only people who really benefited were villagers along the route, but even they lived for many years in continuous fear of raiding parties from Canada, who could have used this as a most convenient access into upper Vermont.

The tiny hamlet of East Craftsbury is located close to this road, although it's unlikely that any raiding party would ever have gained much from attacking the stoical Calvinists who used to populate the area. I visited the church there, a stern Presbyterian building painted dark brown with a fine collection of curved pews inside. It was very quiet, as is this whole region. I picked up a little typed sheet headed "Concerns of the Body," under which were listed people or problems requiring the community's prayer. At the bottom was this rather sad line: "Pray for our young people, who are away at school." Will they ever come back to live and work in this lovely countryside—or will their places be taken by the Sterling students, whose families in many cases are city dwellers to the south? That would indeed be a strange irony.

20. MILAN TO GREENSBORO BEND
A Long Mountain Drive

I woke at about six on a chilly fall morning in Milan, looked out of my camper window and could see absolutely nothing. It was light—light enough to read by—but the fog was so thick that it even enveloped the tree I'd parked beside the night before. Somewhere out there, a few yards away, was the Androscoggin River. I could hear its lazy lapping on the small rocky beach where I had eaten dinner and watched the sunset reflected in its smooth-flowing waters.

Half an hour or so later, after my first morning coffee, strange things began to happen in the fog. A shiny speck, a tiny ball of light, first appeared on the opposite side of the river. Slowly, very slowly, the fog began to lose its chilling whiteness and take on a golden glow. Vague shapes began to emerge—first the tree, its trunk and lower branches flecked with gold; then the rocks on the beach; then the river. After a few minutes, away on the far bank I could make out a line of dark shrouds, the edge of the pine forest. Above I could see small patches of blue sky. The river now appeared to be steaming, like a great cauldron. Shafts of golden sunlight moved and flickered and tiny drops of dew, dangling in silver cobwebs by the river, flashed brilliantly.

Christine Lake

And then, suddenly, the fog was gone. All that remained was a few misty shreds floating over the river or entangled in the dark pines. When I ate breakfast a few minutes later, the scene was filled with all the fresh color of morning.

The short, scenic drive west from Milan, over Milan Hill and past Cedar Pond, leads to Route 110 and a magnificent alpine valley. To the left are the northernmost peaks of the White Mountains National Forest grouped around Mount Cabot (4160 feet); to the right, a cluster of lower hills, the Percy Peaks.

There are two ways through the valley. Route 110 is a fast, well-designed road that provides excellent views of mountain scenery; alternatively there's the old road, a rough one, that passes through a couple of tiny villages and, if you know what to look for, provides access to some splendid tracks into the northern mountains. For example, just past the large barn at Percy there's a path that climbs abruptly into the forest for half a mile or so and then divides. The route straight ahead is normally posted **PRIVATE**, but the short spur to the left leads to a small beach at Christine Lake. There are few stretches of water in New England that can match the beauty of this lake, set in a natural mountain basin and enclosed on all sides by deep woods. Even during the height of summer, cooling breezes roll down from the hills at the far end, rippling the surface of the lake and rustling leaves in the trees around the beach.

It's still wild country around here. I remember one occasion when I was driving through Percy late at night. Just outside the village is the local trash dump, partially concealed from the road. I had my full beams on as I passed the entrance and caught a fleeting glimpse of strange black shapes moving about. I stopped, backed up and pointed the headlights directly into the dump. And there, groping through the crates, cans, bottles and boxes in search of supper, was a family of bears. It's questionable who was more alarmed. The two small cubs ran straight to their mother. I flung the gearstick into reverse as the father gave one of those loud, teethy growls. I dimmed the lights and started to move slowly backward. Fortunately that seemed to satisfy him as to my nonaggressive intentions; after giving me a final fearsome grimace he rejoined his family, and they moved off slowly into the forest. The following day I spoke with residents of the valley about the incident. They assured me that some of the local bears were regarded almost as household pets, and beguiled me with stories of moose and mountain lions, both of which are said to inhabit the area.

The old road follows the meanderings of the river westward from Percy. It briefly touches the main route at Stark, a charming mountain village, complete with covered bridge, set below a great gray cliff, the Devil's Slide. Then it loops away again, passing through woods that slowly give way to a more open landscape of cultivated fields. Seen from the flat

Stark

valley the surrounding mountains are even more dramatic, particularly the two Percy Peaks, whose firm profiles are contrasted sharply behind the tall, smoking chimneys of Groveton. Situated on the Connecticut River, this is not a very prepossessing settlement; yet those who take the trouble to drive through its rather dusty streets will find some unusual architectural influences, such as roofed terraces reminiscent of frontier buildings in the lumber country of northern California, Oregon and Washington.

A few miles to the south this cross-country route passes through the community of Guildhall on the Vermont side of the Connecticut River.

The village seems to have experienced recent decline—there are a number of abandoned properties—yet the green with its ancient maples retains its pastoral charm and boasts one of the most finely detailed library buildings in northern Vermont. Actually, if one takes into account the tumultuous history of this tiny community, it's amazing that anything at all remains. Firstly the villagers had to withstand savage Indian attacks, followed, during the Revolution, by the equally vicious raids of Tory loyalists. In addition, according to old records, settlers were continually harassed by wild animals from the mountains—bears, wolves,

Fountain of flowers—Guildhall

lions—by flooding of the adjacent river and by various unusual plagues, such as the "army of worms," creatures with "a stripe upon the back like black velvet," which arrived in July 1770 and virtually smothered the area. Whole fields were totally covered by masses of slowly crawling shapes. The summer crops stood no chance—"wheat and corn disappeared before them as by magic"—and the worms' regimentation of movement was so precise that "they would go up the side of a house and over it in such a compact column that nothing of boards or shingles could be seen." In September of the same year they vanished as quickly as they had come; but the poor villagers had no time to recover before a plague of pigeons descended upon the community and began to devour everything the worms had missed. At this point the history gets a little obscure, but it appears that the resourceful residents hired "an old gun which took a pound of powder and an equally large quantity of shot" and fired it directly into a field full of the marauding pigeons. Not one bird was killed, but the pigeons vanished, leaving behind "thirty bushel baskets full of legs and toes"!

Somehow the settlers put up with all these disasters. As the size of local cemeteries would suggest, the area was well populated during the eighteenth and nineteenth centuries. The old north cemetery, on Route 102 just outside the village, is particularly interesting to collectors of gravestone inscriptions. In common with many New England burial grounds there are a remarkable number of children's graves. One verse, on the gravestone of Nancy Carlisle (seventeen months and two days) is particularly memorable:

When the archangels trump shall call
And souls to bodies join:
What crowds will wish their lives on earth
Have been as short as mine

Close by is a brief but touching inscription for a young lady of twenty-four:

> Like the folding up of the rose
> She passed away

In recent years a number of people have written books on the inscriptions in New England graveyards. I must admit that when I first began my travels I found it difficult to share the curious enthusiasm of these authors. But since then I have amassed a sizable collection of my own, including these favorites.

From a grave on the green in Glastonbury, Connecticut:

> Here lies one wh
> os life's thrads
> cut asunder she
> was strucke dead
> by a clap of thundr

From the grave of an English cooper in Winslow, Maine:

> Now food for worms
> Like an old rum puncheon
> Marked, numbered and shooked

Then this solemn warning from the grave of a fifteen-year-old girl in Westport, Connecticut:

> Young friends regard this solemn truth,
> Soon you may die like me in youth:
> Death is a debt to nature due,
> Which I have paid and so must you

And finally, in Pelham, Massachusetts, this blunt inscription for a man whose brother claimed he had been poisoned by his wife:

> WARREN GIBBS
> DIED OF ARSENIC POISONING
> MARCH 23RD, 1860
>
> Think my friends when this you see
> How my wife hath dealt by me
> She in some oysters did prepare
> Some poison for my lot . . .

The long inscription goes on to give name and details of this accused murderess!

A mile or so beyond the north cemetery at Guildhall a cross-country road leaves Route 102 at the beautifully maintained Crawford Farm, and immediately climbs high into the mountains. After some arduous driving the crest comes into view, with wide panoramas of the valleys and ranges to the west. Note the lumberjack-style cook shack just by the side of the road, the central focus of the famous Holiday in the Hills Fair and Festival held every year during the last weekend in September. This popular event, attended by thousands, began in a most unusual way a couple of decades ago. Apparently the nearby mountain communities of Granby, Gallup Mills and Victory felt they were being ignored by state authorities. They were particularly outraged to find that they were the only villages in Vermont without electricity. Furthermore, it was learned, plans had been approved to close the post office at Granby. This was too much, and the villagers promptly decided to put this little-known part of the state well and truly on the map before they were officially declared nonexistent.

The Granby town clerk, Maude Lund, whose family has lived in the vicinity for seven generations, came up with the idea of an annual festival built loosely around a lumbering theme, as timber is one of the area's staple products. It began in rather a minor way. Then the efforts of local residents were given prominence in the national media and captured the imagination of the public at large. People flocked in from all over the country to enjoy the festival, with its flea market, horse-pulling and log-cutting contests, antique auctions and the vast lumberjack dinners, served family-style at the cook shack.

Now the festival is a major event, and the funds derived go toward maintaining the schools and churches in the area. Maude Lund, who is still town clerk, is particularly proud of the renovated one-room school just outside Granby. I sat with her in her kitchen one warm fall afternoon a couple of weeks before the festival, and she insisted at least half a dozen times during our chat that I visit the school: "You mustn't miss it. Y'see, we did that. All the people living 'round here did that—we did it all by ourselves. 'Twas the only way, y'see."

Maude Lund's home—Granby

Maude's house is set on a hillside overlooking the beautiful Moose River Valley. A huge cast iron stove sits squarely in the middle of the living room, and on this day the kitchen was filled to overflowing with canning jars. Outside, Maude pointed to a little white star nailed to the wall above the front door and explained that it marked the height of the snowline one particularly bad winter a few years ago. She smiled and added, " 'Twas lucky, I was away at the time!"

Just beyond Granby, a tiny cluster of white buildings, is a fork in the road. Straight ahead it eventually descends to the Passumpsic Valley and winds through the villages of East Burke, Sutton and Sheffield to South Wheelock. If you choose this route, try to include a short detour north to Lake Willoughby. The view from its southern end is one of the most dramatic in the Northeast Kingdom.

The alternative route from the fork leads down into the Victory Bog region, a mountain-enclosed swampland recently designated a wildlife protection area. There are a few trails into the bog, but most are unmarked; newcomers to the area should be cautioned about unsupervised exploration. It's a primitive landscape, and rather dangerous for those not used to walking in swampy terrain.

At North Concord the track joins Interstate 2, but after a few miles west it's possible to make a detour through the rolling countryside to Lyndon, where the last section of this cross-country trip begins. The road swings off westward past the covered bridge and starts a long climb through a wooded valley to rejoin the other fork road at South Wheelock. This is rather different from the countryside around Granby or in the Percy Peaks area—less dramatic, a more gentle, rolling landscape. There are more people living here too, but this time not in pretty white cottages—rather in conditions of dire poverty. There are lopsided shacks hidden in bushes, rusting mobile homes surrounded by bits of automobiles, long lines of washing strung between trees, mangy dogs and half-dressed children. Not many travelers use this stretch of road, so few are aware of the conditions existing in these hills that look so beautiful from the main highway.

I sat one evening above the pathetic, straggling community of Greensboro Bend. A child without shoes or shirt approached me nervously and stood watching just beyond arm's reach. I asked him if he'd like something to eat. He nodded his head, so I made him a thick meat sandwich and gave him a small bottle of soda. He sat down in the dust by the side of the track and began munching. Rarely have I seen jaws move so fast. In a few minutes everything was gone, including the child, although he soon reappeared with his younger sister and a little dog who walked with its tail perpetually between its legs. So out came the supplies again and we all sat down at the side of the path eating more sandwiches.

This last section of the Milan–Greensboro Bend cross-country route is a sobering journey—not particularly pleasant, but one that provides yet another dimension of life in northern New England.

21. PITTSBURG AND VICINITY
New England's Frontier Republic

It was a dismal day in St. Johnsbury, Vermont. Now, a dismal day in St. Johnsbury is truly a dismal day, particularly if the Maple Syrup Museum is closed. So I called a friend and asked him: if he were stuck in St. Johnsbury, where would he go?

"Try the Republic," he said.

There was a pause. "Pardon?" I said.

"The Republic, the area around Pittsburg."

"Pittsburg where?" I asked.

"Pittsburg, New Hampshire, south of Happy Hollow."

"Happy Hollow?"

"I thought you'd traveled New England."

"So did I," I replied.

But as it turned out his advice was well founded, and I dedicate this chapter to my friend, who saved me from that dismal day in St. Johnsbury.

The story of the Indian Stream Republic possesses all the farce and romance of a comic opera, while reflecting the intolerance of a nation whose independence had been gained through revolution only a few years previously. Following the last major clash between the United States and Britain, during the War of 1812, various sections of the Canadian/American boundary had been left undefined. In what is now the northernmost tip of New Hampshire, many of the four hundred or so inhabitants felt no overwhelming allegiance to either country. So in April 1829 they held a meeting at the local schoolhouse—afterward named Independence Hall—and declared themselves to be "The United Citizens of the Indian Stream Territory"; later, in July 1832, the area was proudly renamed the Republic of Indian Stream. This was no casual affair. The zealous citizens drew up a bill of rights and a constitution, and created an electoral body that happened to include the entire voting population. At first neither the Canadian nor American government seemed to treat the situation very seriously, and, according to the Official Coos County History, the citizens of the Republic lived under idyllic conditions:

> Neither state nor county taxes were levied—there was no law for the prevention or punishment of crime, the enforcement of civil contracts or any of the multi-form necessities of civil commerce for which human governments are instituted. Private schools were supported by subscription, roads were cut through the forest and improved by voluntary contribution of labor; and

school houses were built in the same manner. There was but little crime. Everyone found work enough to do in clearing up the forests and provided for the wants of his family. . . . There was but little money and most of the necessities of life were produced at home. Barter was an important factor in trade but little credit was given. The payment of debts was a matter of honor. . . .

Unfortunately the quality of life in the Republic soon deteriorated, and tensions began to rise. The United States government imposed duties on all goods exported from the tiny principality, and the Canadian government attempted to enforce its draft laws on the reluctant populace. Also, local crime began to increase, which persuaded the citizens to seek stronger laws of their own.

Both the Canadians and the Americans were now anxious to take over the area. Eventually, following a series of skirmishes, the brief Indian Stream War settled the issue in favor of the United States, and the New Hampshire militia occupied the territory until details of the American conquest were finalized. Many settlers of the Republic left in disgust following its official dissolution in 1840. Some went into Canada; others, including Luther Parker, ex-president of the Republic, moved out west—where later Parker's son was elected lieutenant governor of Wisconsin.

An idiosyncrasy!—Canaan

Beaver Brook Falls—near Stewartstown Hollow

The area was renamed Pittsburg. Today this 360-square-mile township (the largest in New Hampshire) still has a frontier flavor. Its pine forests, following every undulation of the hilly countryside, were, until most of the full-grown timber was felled, the home of scores of lumber camps. Communities such as Canaan, situated just over the Vermont border alongside the embryonic Connecticut River, possess a character reminiscent of Old West towns—elaborately detailed wooden mansions juxtaposed with flimsy false-front buildings and the occasional architectural idiosyncrasy! The town of Pittsburg, however, is a rather nondescript community whose only notable feature is a well-preserved covered bridge at its southern entrance. To the north is the tiny village of Happy Hollow (yes, there is indeed a Happy Hollow, and I apologize to my friend for doubting his word), but, other than another covered bridge, there's little here of note. In fact the last time I visited, the whole place, a grand total of three cottages, was up for sale!

What makes this northern portion of New Hampshire memorable is not so much its communities but the fine series of lakes that stretch northward from Pittsburg. With the exception of Back Lake, just outside the town, the other major bodies of water—Lake Frances, First Connecticut Lake and Second Lake—are largely undeveloped; but best of all for the traveler seeking solitude are the tiny ponds hidden in the mountains close to the Canadian border. Although their names (Pond Number One, Third Lake, Fourth Lake) are not particularly inspiring, and access even on foot can be difficult, they are some of New Hampshire's most beautiful and are well worth a trek up the mountains.

Route 145 south from Pittsburg to the old lumbering town of Colebrook is a most rewarding drive. It passes across the 45th parallel—a point precisely equidistant from the North Pole and the Equator. An interesting side trip, down a rough track just north of Stewartstown Hollow, is the North Hill Cemetery. It is here that Metallak, "Lone Indian of the Magalloway," is buried. During his day he was a well-loved local figure who, following the onset of blindness after a hunting incident, was taken in by the residents of Stewartstown and became a public charge until his death in 1847 at (if the records are correct) the age of one hundred and twenty. His skill as a hunter was such that even after his blindness he continued to make expeditions to his beloved Umbagog Lake, where his wife, Molly, was buried, and on one occasion acted as a guide for Governor Enoch Lincoln of Maine, one of his many admirers.

A few miles farther to the south a small clearing at the side of the road reveals this splendid scene—Beaver Brook falling in a series of leaping cascades more than two hundred feet into the valley below.

Colebrook, at the confluence of the Mohawk and Connecticut Rivers, is a substantial town; yet like many towns in the region it still possesses that distinctive frontier flavor. As the sketch (page 126) shows, this segment of the town's main street could just as easily be in Nevada, Arizona or northern California. Old photographs in the Colebrook library show how little the character of the place has changed in the past seventy years. However, what is startling is the change in the landscape within the

Main street—Colebrook

same period. At the turn of the century this was real lumber country—the hills and mountains around, for as far as one could see, were as bare as the sand hills of Nebraska. The felled timber logs roared down the Connecticut River through the town followed by the burly lumberjacks, who, according to a local historian/journalist, "rode the head of the writhing brown serpent from its spawning grounds in the forest of the north to its death throes in the sawmills by the sea."

Colebrook endured largely because its own economy was diversified and not entirely dependent on the lumber trade. It is said that there was a brief flurry of gold mining on the slopes of Mount Monadnock just across the Connecticut River. Medicinal springs were discovered in the same area and ambitious plans were drawn up for parks, baths and bottling plants. But when the elaborate Nirvana Hotel was destroyed by a hurricane in 1893 before it even opened, interest waned in such projects, and the area concentrated on developing its dairy and potato industries. It was the latter venture that brought almost as much wealth to the region as lumber, for the potato was a versatile plant—and particularly valuable in the preparation of starch and whiskey.

Visitors to this region who arrive from Vermont, as I did, should take the drive eastward through mighty Dixville Notch. A pause at the magnificent

Balsams Resort is recommended. This is one of the last remaining examples in the area of the great mountain resorts built during the early nineteenth century, when the rapid construction of railroads opened up the previously inaccessible White Mountains and other ranges to the wealthy in the cities to the south. This pantile-roofed complex set in the heart of "America's Switzerland," and looking for all the world like one of those large Victorian hotels on the shores of Lake Lucerne, is said to have been built on land owned by Daniel Webster. It was the brainchild of Henry Hale, an inventor who gained an overnight fortune selling his revolving-chair patent to George Pullman, of Pullman-car fame. Even though the resort's fortunes have fluctuated considerably over the years, it still manages to survive in what is without doubt the most scenic location in the northern mountains of New England.

After the long descent to the rather bedraggled community of Errol, there is one last drive—known as the 13 Mile Woods—that should not be missed. The route follows the Androscoggin River southward to the paper-manufacturing city of Berlin. The drive begins just outside Errol. The placid river, with occasional flurries of rapids, meanders through dark forests of conifers. The landscape is totally wild yet offers, in contrast to the dramatic pinnacles and crags of Dixville Notch, a mood of great calm and peace. It's a beautiful way to end the journey through the Indian Stream Republic.

Dixville Notch

# Region III: Maine

Old fire station—Damariscotta

22. THE BRISTOL PENINSULA
Pemaquid, Pirates and Lobster Pots

The Bristol Peninsula attracts its share of summer tourists, particularly the camera buffs, who hurry down Route 130 to magnificent Pemaquid Point, snap a few pictures and hurry back up to Route 1 for another "experience" somewhere else along the coast. Fortunately it's a big enough region to absorb these and other summer groups without changing its essential qualities. There are miles upon miles of rough country lanes rarely used, tiny fishing villages rarely visited and beautiful ponds rarely noticed. The area is full of history, so much so that this essay can hardly claim to do more than provide readers with a brief glimpse of the Pemaquid heritage.

The peninsula really starts south of Route 1 and the unusually charming communities of Damariscotta and Waldoboro. I sketched this onetime fire station in Damariscotta, which possesses a number of fine old wooden buildings, including the 1754 Chapman/Hall House (open to the public) at the top end of Main Street.

Waldoboro, with its rather stern brick business district, has an interesting early history. In 1748 the owner of the township, General Samuel Waldo, induced a group of Germans to settle here with extravagant promises and descriptions of the area. A little note on one of the cemetery headstones tells the story simply:

> This town was settled in 1748 by Germans
> who immigrated to this place with the
> promise and expectation of finding a
> prosperous city, instead of which they
> found nothing but wilderness.

Although many of the original settlers moved out in disgust, some remained and founded the first Lutheran meeting house in Maine in 1772. It still stands today a short distance south of the town on Route 32, one of the many early churches scattered throughout the peninsula.

From excavations in the fields around the reconstructed Fort William Henry, located near Pemaquid Point at the southern tip of the peninsula, it would appear that Pemaquid was settled even before the first British immigrants gained their official foothold on the New England coast during the 1620s. Champlain noted a community here on his 1605 charting voyage, and a few years later, in 1614, Captain John Smith described a port called Pemaquid "in the Maine" opposite Monhegan. Some observers have speculated that the remains may be of a Viking settlement, but more informed researchers believe this was a small trading base for merchants from Bristol, England—although they find it hard to explain the unusual stone-paved streets, the massively built walls and the "fairy pipes" found scattered around the site. English folklore suggests that these tiny tobacco pipes were made especially for fairies, goblins and the like, and were normally left each evening by the fireplace for their use!

The fort's long and complex history must make it one of the most disputed settlements along the Maine coast, although its beginnings were

Fort William Henry and excavations

New Harbor

unusually civilized. In 1622 the Indian Samoset allowed the Pilgrims to use his supply of corn at Pemaquid to avoid starvation. In gratitude the Pilgrims purchased the land (instead of just taking it), and when it was resold in 1625 to a John Brown of Monhegan the first legal property deed ever prepared in New England was signed and witnessed here. There's a granite marker at New Harbor commemorating the event. A fort was built in 1630, but soon after, one of the coast's innumerable pirates, Dixey Bull, raided the garrison and village with no difficulty. Later, in 1676, relations with the Indians deteriorated and the fort was destroyed by a local tribe who had joined the famous chief King Philip in his ill-fated struggle to rid the East Coast of colonists (see "The Great Rhode Island Swamp"—page 36). Fortunately the citizens were warned and all escaped; but in 1689 they were not so lucky, and many died when the Indians, encouraged by the French, destroyed the settlement again.

Three years later yet another fort was built under the direction of Sir William Phips, then governor of Massachusetts, only to be destroyed by the French this time in the person of Baron de Castin, whose cannons in 1696 bombarded the battlements and gained an early surrender. English domination of Maine east of the Kennebec River was thus ended for almost seventy years, during that long period of conflict known as the French and Indian Wars. The area still attracted settlers, however, and another fort was built in 1729. But conditions remained bloody, particularly in the 1740s, when Indian attacks were vicious and regular. Finally, after all these efforts to maintain an effective stronghold against attack, the settlers themselves destroyed the fort to prevent it from falling into British hands during the American Revolution. The site was abandoned until 1893, when the Pemaquid Improvement Association was formed to raise funds for the partial reconstruction of the fort as a memorial. The project was finally undertaken as a state park in 1908; a museum was later built to display excavation findings.

Today the peninsula is a quiet corner of the coast, possessing three beautiful fishing villages in New Harbor, Round Pond and Pemaquid. The first, with its high wharves, mounds of lobster pots and huddled groups of trawlers, is a photographer's dream, especially when seen from the narrow road along the south side of the harbor. My favorite view here is from the old green bench under the fir tree just past the seafood company on the north side. There's also a recently opened restaurant nearby where on warm summer nights you can sit on the terrace overlooking the inlet and crack lobsters, dipping their firm flesh into hot drawn butter. (Travelers should note that they can take day trips to Monhegan Island from this harbor.)

A little farther up the east side of the peninsula is Round Pond. Like Tenants Harbor (see "Monhegan"—page 142), it was once a well-known granite-mining center, and sloops would sail directly into the quarry for loading. Just north of the village is the Old Rock Schoolhouse, constructed almost entirely of large granite blocks. Today Round Pond is a lobstering community with some boat-building activity and a most unusual collection of mansard-roofed houses. Nobody seems to know why this style became so popular here, although it could have been due to the early French dominance. This tiny home is my favorite. I have never before seen such a small building with this kind of roof.

A mile or so out in Muscongus Bay, directly across from Round Pond, is Loud's Island. This attractive little splinter of land has quite a history. It is officially classified "unorganized territory," but in many respects its citizens have been, and still are, so independent that "republic" might be a better name. In the mid-1700s an erratic government survey omitted to mention the existence of the island, thus indirectly pronouncing it and its population stateless. Nevertheless the town of Bristol considered the island to be within its boundaries and carefully ensured that taxes were paid. Then, surprisingly, in the national elections of 1860, Loud's Island residents voted solidly Democratic in this Republican territory. The Bristol selectmen, in order to avoid any upset of their favorite candidates, declared that if the island was really nonexistent according to the maps, then its votes were also nonexistent. They promptly refused to include them in the count, thus assuring the success of the Republican candidates.

The islanders, outraged, almost declared themselves an independent nation, but instead made do with a terse statement of intent: "We are willing to support the United States, but not the town of Bristol." So the island remained "unorganized"—and that's just fine with the few inhabitants, who live an undisturbed life, rarely troubled by tourists or any of the larger concerns of the mainland.

Mansard-roofed house
—Round Pond

Bristol Mills

The back roads that meander through this central portion of the peninsula make delightful driving. The woods are thick but every so often there's a view—an open field, an old farmhouse, a small, still pond. A number of these roads meet at Bristol Mills, where I made this sketch of a towerless church. The tower sits in an adjoining field; last time I was there, it seemed to be used as a henhouse!

For contrast to the seabound beauty of Bristol, drive north on Route 1 into the rolling forest and farmland of Jefferson and Whitefield Townships. There are some remarkable views on Route 213 of long Damariscotta Lake, particularly from Bunker Hill. The whole region has a totally unspoiled flavor, as though nothing has really changed for the last hundred years or so. An old guidebook describes Jefferson as "a community of comfortably rambling farm houses." Similarly the villages of Whitefield, Head Tide, Alna and Sheepscot are perfect examples of New England settlements. The white wooden homes are clustered together along narrow streets shaded by trees, in total harmony with the landscape. Interesting examples of old churches and schoolhouses can be found in abundance, and just outside Jefferson there's one of the region's last remaining cattle pounds. At nearby Cooper's Mill is a specially constructed salmon run enabling the spawning fish to negotiate a rather high dam in the Sheepscot River.

These two segments of the region, the peninsula south of Route 1 and the farming area to the north around Damariscotta Lake, are very different in landscape, and yet each expresses something of Maine's varied character. By all means take the obligatory photograph of the lighthouse at Pemaquid Point—but then wander the country lanes at a slow, easy pace, enjoying all the little-known nooks and crannies.

23. MONHEGAN
Journey to a Small Island

"It gets bad in winter when those westerlies blow off the islands."

Captain Earl Field took over the wheel from his copilot, pulled his broad-brimmed cap down sharply and stared ahead through the spray at the gray profile of Monhegan Island, "backed like a whale," in the distance. The little ferryboat had just left calm waters, through a scattering of pine-covered islands off Port Clyde, and had begun to bounce on the heavy swell. There were six miles of open ocean to cross before we reached the quiet lee of the island's harbor. Earl seemed to regard the bouncing, which had sent most of his spray-drenched passengers scurrying for the enclosed rear compartment of the boat, as average for late fall: "Come back 'round January, and I'll show you some real riding. It's gonna be a rough winter." He paused to adjust course a little as a sudden gust of icy wind blew us almost broadside to the oncoming waves. "Once went two years without missing a trip. Was pretty pleased about that." He allowed himself a flicker of a smile, a brief twinkle, and then his

Harbor scene—Monhegan

face regained its dour expression as he kept the boat headed for the distant gap between Monhegan and its tiny companion island, Manana.

Earl has been making the island trip twice a day in the summer, three times a week in the winter, for more than thirty years. His mailboat ferry, the *Laura B,* is a tough little lady. Beyond a few creaks, heavy seas don't seem to bother her at all; so long as Earl keeps heading in the right direction she purrs along without complaint. It's only the passengers or the occasional live cargo that creates a fuss. On the day I made the crossing there were two poor dogs who, at one point in the turbulent journey, stood dripping wet and frozen at the edge of the boat apparently contemplating a joint suicide until rescued by their equally wet and frozen owners. Even more unhappy was a boxful of kittens, who mewed and cried continuously throughout the journey, much to the distress of their young owner: "They just won't stop—I've tried everything." Her explanation didn't seem to satisfy a group of large ladies from the mainland, who regarded the girl and her noisy package disdainfully for most of the voyage.

Earl laughingly remarked, "We've carried just about every kind of cargo you can imagine," and went on to tell me of the goats, raccoons, sheep and even deer that had made the eleven-mile crossing from Port Clyde to the island, which depends on these ferryboats for all its supplies (boats also leave from Bar Harbor and New Harbor).

In this respect Monhegan is a true Maine island—tenuously linked to the land yet proudly independent—unlike many of the more popular places immediately off the coast where tourists and summer residents have reduced the art of island living to a vacation pastime.

A resident population of less than one hundred continues its lobster fishing in the short season (January 1 through June 25). During a good year it can be a profitable venture, although in recent times hauls have fluctuated wildly due to increased local pollution and more intensive lobster-catching methods used in the deeper waters at the edge of the continental shelf. Nevertheless the tradition continues, and all other island occupations seem insignificant by comparison.

This tiny forest-covered, mist-shrouded land, approximately one and a half miles by half a mile, has a longer history than most other parts of the United States. Strange rock inscriptions on neighboring Manana are considered by many historians to be Viking grafitti—a few scribbled notes made by the wandering Norsemen who sailed along the New England coast around A.D. 1000; and more recently, at the time of John Cabot's brief visit in 1497, Monhegan Island is thought to have been a popular resting and repair center for European fishermen—Portuguese, Spanish, English and Basque. Verrazano, the Italian navigator/explorer, makes repeated reference to the island in his charting notes of 1524. In 1605, Captain George Weymouth harbored his vessel *Archangel* here long enough for his crew to collect supplies of fresh water, and for the captain to perform a flag-and-cross-raising ceremony for the benefit of the British crown. Weymouth later made friends with the mainland Indians, only to destroy their faith soon afterward by kidnapping five members of the tribe and hauling them off to London for public exhibition. This was but the first of a long series of stupid acts by insensitive British explorers, and it's little wonder that the Maine tribes eventually tired of such treacheries and joined the French (who were far more sympathetic to the native culture) in their efforts to oust all British settlers.

Other visitors to the island during the same period included Bartholomew Gosnold (see "Cuttyhunk Island"—page 44), Champlain and finally Captain John Smith, who stayed long enough in 1614 to build seven ships and to plant a garden "on top of the rocky isle . . . in May that grew so well that it served for sallets [salads] in June and July." Later residents of Monhegan obviously had a high regard for Captain Smith; they erected a bronze plaque near the schoolhouse to commemorate the tercentenary of his arrival in the tiny harbor.

Permanent settlement of the island began as early as 1619, and by the time the Pilgrims arrived Monhegan's prosperity was such that the inhabitants gladly assisted the newer colonies in their efforts to establish themselves farther down the coast. Even during the early years of the French and Indian Wars in Maine, Monhegan remained a thriving bastion of trade—although by 1676 the conflict had finally spread to the island, and it was abandoned for almost a hundred years. Later it revived again under the influence of a series of owner families—the Trefethrens, Horns and Starlings—but it never regained its former importance. The coastal ports now dominated New England trade, and Monhegan became a quiet enclave for fishermen and, much later, for a colony of artists and writers started by Rockwell Kent. Until recently there was also a resident hermit, Ray Phillips (immortalized in Yolla Niclas' book *The Island Shepherd*), who died a few weeks prior to my visit. He lived in a ramshackle hillside dwelling on Manana and rowed, once a week, across the harbor to pick up supplies from the store in Monhegan. Then once a year, according to local residents, he would journey to the mainland "for a bath and a night on the town" (in that sequence!). I asked Captain Earl about his replacement.

"No problem there, there's another on the island already. Yessir, we've got ourselves a twenty-year-old hermit this time." Whether the new hermit will last as long as Mr. Phillips remains to be seen. According to Earl, he had lived on Manana for at least fifty years and was eighty-three when he died—"One night his lamp wasn't lit so we knew he'd gone."

As the *Laura B* nears the island it passes the two seal ledges, often populated by a score or more of these barking mammals during the summer, and moves into calmer waters. The passengers, mostly young, many with beards, gather at the bow and watch in almost reverent silence as the boat pulls slowly into the narrow harbor. Above on the steep hillside are clusters of gray buildings—simple wooden homes, lobster sheds, a school, the hotel and, right at the top, a lighthouse. There are mounds of lobster pots everywhere—between the houses, on the wharves, beside the little unpaved tracks that meander up from the harbor and disappear around curves in the hillside. Suddenly the silence is broken: "John, is Mary with you?" "Dianne, have you got the cats?" "Did

Hermit's shack—Manana

Street scene—Monhegan

they deliver the milk, Earl?" "Where are my canvases?" "Tighten that rope!" "Is the Peterson party there?" Even the dogs forget their previous malaise and join in the general hullaballoo with loud, thankful barks.

For a brief interval the harbor and lower village are a flurry of activity. Then, almost as quickly as it was shattered, there is silence again. Newcomers are soon absorbed into the island, off along its numerous paths and trails. As no camping is allowed, because of the very real danger of fires, visitors must either find themselves a room at a hotel or boardinghouse (reservations are often made months in advance) or return to the mainland on the last ferry of the day.

Fortunately, because of its size most of the island can be seen in a day at a leisurely pace. In the village itself are numerous scenes such as this, to keep photographers and artists enraptured for hours. For the more adventurous there are great headlands on the "far" side, which on stormy days throw up sea spray to amazing heights. These cliffs are linked to the village by a series of narrow trails, some of which pass through the Cathedral Woods, strangely silent even on a busy summer day. Footsteps are muffled by the deep carpet of pine needles. Ferns and tiny flowers (over six hundred species of plants have been identified on the island) are scattered over the hillside, and the occasional cry of a seagull filters through with the sunlight.

It's one of those places that remains in the memory, to be called on when needed. Even day visitors, after their few brief hours on the island, return to the mainland a little quieter in spirit. There's something about these woods, the tiny community and its slow pace of life, the cliffs and those vistas of the Atlantic as it rolls over a hundred horizons to the coast of Spain, that affects almost everyone who visits Monhegan. As a young bearded and blue-jeaned artist told me on the outward crossing, "I first came out here about five years ago, just for a day—y'know, two cameras, miles of film, rush, rush, rush. But I didn't take any photographs, didn't make any sketches. All I did was just sit up by the lighthouse and listen to the island. Since then—well, it's the only place I ever come to. Every chance I get to leave Boston, I'm here. It's all I need."

Travelers who take the Port Clyde–Monhegan boat should allow time, either before or after the visit to the island, to explore the narrow mainland peninsula linking Rockland and Route 1 with the ferry. Although some signs of new development—of the summer-cottage variety—are evident, the area is largely uncommercialized. Tiny villages such as St. George, Spruce Head, Tenants Harbor, Long Cove and Ash Point are dotted along its length. Many, like Port Clyde itself, are lobster-fishing communities with high wooden wharves, ramshackle storage sheds and piles of pots and brightly colored floats. Inside the small dockside warehouses are the lobster tanks, usually brimming with hundreds of these claw-waving delicacies. There's a particularly large series of eighteen tanks in a building on the wharf at Spruce Head, a mile or so beyond the Lobster Lane Bookshop. It's not hard to find. The lobster bait of rotting fish is normally "matured" in vats outside the building—the stench is far-reaching and quite distinct!

There are plenty of back roads on the peninsula. In most cases they lead to tiny inlets and coves or, in the case of some near Tenants Harbor, into old granite quarries. I visited one, just past the lobster pound at Tenants Harbor, where the main quarry had filled with clear fresh water to form a marvelous, if somewhat deep, swimming hole. It was obviously a favorite spot with the locals. The edge of the pond was littered with lobster shells, six inches deep in places.

One back road leads to the Old Homestead Museum, a project of the Mussel Ridge Historical Society. A tiny, shingle-faced cottage, typical of Maine coastal dwellings in the early 1800s, has been restored, and the rooms are being refurbished in the domestic character of that period.

It's a beautiful area to explore, and since the peninsula is so narrow it's almost impossible to get lost. So take any track not marked as private or a dead end and you are sure to come across scenes such as this—a lobster shack somewhere near Ash Point. The sea is ever present: a brief flicker of sun on a narrow inlet, a glimpse between trees or, without warning, a broad vista of the Atlantic, dotted with islands, their conifer-covered backs silhouetted against a bright blue sky or blazing sunset. Always islands; wherever you look there are islands, and out there in the hazy distance is the "High Round Isle," the "Whaleback," the small world that is Monhegan.

Lobster shack—near Ash Point

Old store—near Lubec

24. JONESPORT AND VICINITY
The Unusual Voyage of Pastor Adams

It was late afternoon on the northern Maine coast and I was in a tiny store chatting with a wind-wrinkled old man in a "Maine cap." We had gone through the normal weather/health/inflation sequence and were now embroiled in a subject of great mutual interest—food. I had shown some curiosity about the packages of salted, dried fish piled on the counter between the pantyhose and the chewing tobacco, and asked if he had any idea of how it should be cooked. A brilliant monologue ensued in which the little storeowner presented an almost encyclopedic array of recipes for casseroles, soups and stews, ending with what he considered the most simple and yet the most classic of dishes: fried fish with crisp salt pork strips and boiled potatoes. By this time my gastric juices were flowing unchecked, and I left the store in search of a restaurant he had mentioned that was farther south in the Jonesport area. Fortunately, in the process of satisfying my appetite I also found another delightful hidden corner of the Maine coast.

Jonesport is a small lobster-fishing community at the southern tip of the great Blueberry Barrens of Deblois, Wesley and Whitneyville. Even along the road down the peninsula from Route 1 there are occasional clearings where the forest has been cut back to allow ground-hugging clumps of blueberries to grow in profusion. In fall this drive is spectacular. The tiny blueberry leaves turn deep scarlet and the fields appear to be burning with an intense flameless heat.

The lobster industry of the region, centered around the Jonesport harbors, seems a most carefully structured and controlled business. There is little or no casual labor involved, except in the case of the amateur "lobstermen" who pay their meager license fees and dabble with their fifteen pots off the coast. The professionals—the real lobstermen who fish for a living and who often own more than two hundred pots—have no time for the amateurs. They claim that "the outsiders" have unfairly reduced their livelihood and don't always abide by the strict rules relating to size of catch and seasonal limits. However, many of the locals around Jonesport feel that the lobstermen have nevertheless created a lucrative little industry for themselves.

While sitting on one of the wharves, surrounded by lobster pots and floats, I talked with one young man who had lived in the town most of his life. "They're a crafty bunch," he told me. "They moan and groan about prices and lobster shortages and the Russian trawlers, and all the time they're hauling in the money, hand over fist—and that's only for five months' work. Rest of the year some of them run hotels and restaurants and make another good living off the tourists." Allowing for the bias of my plain-spoken companion, who clearly wished himself in the lobster business, it does appear that the lobstermen of Maine have a good hold on the reins of their own destinies. Lobster canning, which during the mid-1800s dominated most of the industry, had been legislated to death by the end of the century. The lobstermen then amalgamated into cooperatives and began to control their own pounds—where thousands of live lobsters are kept in natural storage until demand and price are satisfactorily high. Storage in the pounds enables the official six-month season to be declared.

Many have praised this move on the part of the lobstermen. Indeed it does serve to safeguard a valuable and scarce resource, and it also helps reduce the nuisance of fishing during the shedding season, when lobsters lose their shells and grow replacements. A shedding or shed lobster is a tasteless creature, unpalatable and unmarketable—so it's a practical solution to leave the fishing until the proportion of shedders in a catch is minimal.

But for all their canny business methods, the lobsterman is still a man of the sea. I watched from the wharf at Jonesport as they cleaned their tiny boats, mended their pots and painted their floats. Even the younger men had wrinkled, bronzed faces, and I thought of what it must be like to be out there on the open sea, often away from the lee of islands, on a sub-zero February morning before dawn with the wind freezing the spray to the deck and rigging, hauling up pot after tedious pot. I concluded that they deserved every dollar they could make!

The scene at Jonesport is typical of most Maine lobstering communities. Boats, bobbing and rocking, are tied to long, rickety wharves supported on huge pine pilings that jut out into the waters of a narrow inlet. Piles of

Harbor scene—Beals Island

pots are stacked along the length of the wharf and on the dockside. There's invariably the aroma of fish mixed with the smell of fresh spruce wafted in by winds from the offshore islands. Scattered along and between the wharves are countless tiny storage shacks, grayed by age and winter storms. And then, on the higher ground overlooking the harbor are white clapboard cottages peering through pines, mingled with larger Victorian mansions. Jonesport possesses some particularly fine examples just around the Congregational church. In fact the whole community has such a mature, sedate feel it's difficult to believe that some of these hardheaded and pragmatic Yankee citizens were once so enamored of a visiting actor/evangelist that they donated all their possessions to his cause and set off on an incredible expedition to establish a religious colony in the Holy Land! The year was 1865. A Mormon elder, George Washington ("Pastor") Adams, traveled the coast around Jonesport selling his religious treatise "The Sword of Truth and the Harbinger of Peace" and persuading residents to join him in an expedition to Jaffa, where he planned to establish a colony "to commence the great work of restoration foretold by the old prophets . . . as well as by our Lord, himself." Either he must have been a remarkably convincing man or recent fishing seasons must have been bad and local Yankee families ready for a change, for in August 1866 he left Maine with 175 followers and after a long voyage arrived in Palestine.

Unfortunately nothing went right. Mr. Adams disappeared after a protracted bout with the bottle, and many of the settlers died of unfamiliar diseases. Some managed to pay their way back, but most were stranded

The Blueberry Barrens

until the New York *Sun* decided the escapade would make a good human interest story and loaned them the money to return. With the exception of one young man, all accepted the offer. He, in typical Yankee fashion, stayed on and made a fortune by running a stage line between Jaffa and Jerusalem!

Recently linked by a bridge to the mainland at Jonesport is nearby Beals Island, a tiny, undulating outcrop of conifer-covered land. Until the coming of the bridge the five hundred or so inhabitants of the island had maintained their own culture, speaking a kind of Elizabethan English dialect. They gave unusual names to the various parts of their island, particularly the rocky ledges exposed at low tide—The Virgin's Breasts, The Lecherous Priest, Drowned Boy's Ledge, Crumple and Mistake. They even possessed their own folk heroes, which included early members of the Beal family who seem to have been graced with incredible physiques. Manwaring Beal, the first settler in 1764, was so enormous that special furniture had to be made for him; and his son, "Long Barney" Beal, apparently carried on the family hallmark. Barney became fabled for his exploits of strength. He is said to have taken on fifteen assailants at one time in a Portland saloon and to have been the only one left standing. Once, harassed by Canadian militia for fishing too close to the border, he broke all their guns over his knee and tossed them into the sea.

Although Jonesport and Beals are the only main settlements in the area, there are plenty of back roads worth exploring in the vicinity of Addison and South Addison. In most cases they end at beautiful coves littered with lobster pots.

For contrast, take a journey north into the Blueberry Barrens, a region with a character all its own. The land is flatter than the rolling terrain of the potato areas to the north (see "Houlton and Vicinity"—page 163) and the picturesque lake country to the east. The forest is less dominant, and the fields often abut directly on the roads across the Barrens, stretching away into the distance—acre upon acre of open land full of blueberries. Although this is still wild country, with none of the conveniences of the coastal area, it's an interesting drive, particularly around Wesley and Deblois, and a welcome relief from the interminable forest-lined roads of the Maine woods.

For most of the year the Barrens is a silent area, with few people to be seen in the fields. The only traffic on "the Airline" (a nickname for Route 9) is trucks and other commercial vehicles utilizing this fast link between Bangor and eastern Maine. Tourists rarely pass this way, as it means sacrificing the magnificent coastal drive. The blueberries grow here naturally, and all the farmers have to do is keep the forest back by "burning over" the fields every three years or so to remove scrub and other intruding vegetation. The burning doesn't seem to affect the blueberry plants adversely; in fact they grow even better the following season.

Still, it's poor country. Although major blueberry-packing companies have bought up many of the marginal farms and have streamlined production and marketing methods, there are still scores of small holdings where families scrabble for a living on three or four acres. Usually they're tucked away down roads off the highway, unknown or unnoticed.

But suddenly in August, the Barrens come alive. Even the small backroad farms are filled with people young and old, wielding strangely shaped comb forks for scooping the berries from the ankle-high bushes. It's back-tearing labor, and yet hundreds of families journey to this region every year to join in the brief, four-week harvest.

Many of the migrant pickers are members of the Micmac Indian tribe, now centered in New Brunswick and Nova Scotia, who say that for them this is the most profitable month of the year. They put up with abominable living conditions for the brief duration of their stay—often sleeping in tarpaper shacks provided by the packing companies with no fresh water, electricity or sanitation facilities. As a much publicized 1974 report of the Maine Human Rights Commission stated, these conditions "are an affront to even the most minimal standards of dignity." However, many of the 1500-odd Micmac pickers, and scores of other families who join in the annual harvest, claim they can put up with such conditions so long as the picking price per box stays high and the fall rains hold off. Well over twenty million pounds of berries are picked in less than one month—then, while the farmers and packers rake in their profits, the migrant workers leave as quickly as they came and scurry northward for the Aroostook potato harvest (see "Houlton and Vicinity"—page 163).

The Barrens, with their broad vistas, fire-colored in the autumn, provide yet one more dimension of the varied scenery that characterizes northern Maine.

Cutler

25. EASTPORT/LUBEC
A Quiet Stretch of Coast, Rich in History

At first I wandered the narrow lanes at a leisurely pace, chatting with fishermen and enjoying the sweeping views of the Atlantic from high cliffs, oblivious to the region's heritage. It was just a very appealing area to travel, to explore. The small coastal towns, such as the lobstering community of Cutler, had a completely unspoiled charm. Life seemed to go on at a steady, civilized pace, and few brows were furrowed. Yet as I began to learn more of the area, tales and legends emerged that I found unusually dramatic and colorful. This seemingly docile corner of Maine was once a robust land—plagued by pirates, invariably at odds with the British, enthusiastically involved in smuggling rackets, visited by talented con men, home of Indians, onetime summer resort of Franklin Delano Roosevelt and, more recently, location of an ambitious scheme employing hundreds to tap the energy generated by the region's incredible thirty-foot tides.

The pleasant waterfront town of Eastport, its steep main street lined with the white clapboard homes of trawler captains, is similarly deceptive. Guidebooks describe Eastport as a once dynamic place; it was "the busiest harbor in the United States" following Jefferson's Embargo Act of 1807, and was captured by the British for a period of four years during the War of 1812. This was one of the great smuggling eras. At a time when Britain and France were embroiled in yet another of their frequent wars, America found her shipping being preyed on by both sides. In addition the British developed an annoying habit of commandeering American sailors at will. So the government decided the only way it could re-

149

Main street—Eastport

taliate was to place an embargo on its own ports and kill all trade relations with France and Britain. It was a hard self-inflicted blow that brought severe economic distress to many of the large coastal cities of Massachusetts and Connecticut—but not to little Eastport. It was only a few minutes' sailing time across Passamaquoddy Bay to the Canadian shore, and trade was brisk. During one week alone, thirty thousand barrels of flour, worth approximately $4 per barrel on the American side, were sold for $16 per barrel to the British on the Canadian side. In addition, there was a $3-per-barrel transportation charge—which of course brought out every bark, barge, trawler, dinghy, canoe and even a raft or two in the Eastport area.

More recently the town, which possesses one of the finest natural harbors on the Atlantic seaboard, was an important fishing and processing center with a wealth of industries, including canning of sardines, shrimp and tuna; production of fish meal, fish oil and pearl essence (from fish scales), and construction of tough little "Bay of Fundy" boats.

Today, unfortunately, Eastport seems to have lost much of its former glory. Many of the long-legged wharves are empty, the canneries are closing and little new industry seems to be coming into the community. Some residents blame it all on the Passamaquoddy Tidal Power Development Project, which began with great fanfare and lavish expenditure in 1935 under the FDR administration and was later revived briefly during the Kennedy era, only to fold again, throwing the local economy into total disarray. Estimates vary, but it appears that the final abandonment of the project led to a loss of almost five thousand local jobs.

For many years the new village of Quoddy, built to house project employees, was left empty, but some of it evidently is now occupied by members of the Passamaquoddy Indian Tribe, whose Pleasant Point Reservation is on the Eastport peninsula. There are about four hundred Indians living on the reservation, and they continue to preserve as well as they can their language and culture. The tribe, part of the larger Algonkian group, was once a member of the vast Wabanaki Confederacy, which included most of the Maine, New Hampshire and Maritime Indians. Their first known contact with whites came in 1604 when Champlain and his company spent the winter on St. Croix Island north of Eastport, near Calais. Champlain's chronicler, Marc Lescarbot, wrote with great respect about the caliber of the local Indians: "They have courage, fidelity, generosity, humanity and hospitality, judgement and good sense; so that if we commonly call them savages the word is abusive and unmerited for they are anything but that."

There was excellent rapport between the French and Indians that winter. One of the chiefs converted to Catholicism, and many others followed. Even the sign at the junction of Routes 1 and 190 that proclaims **WELCOME TO SEBAYICK** (the Pleasant Point Reservation) mentions St. Anne's Mission, founded in 1604, and today most of the remaining tribe is still devoutly Roman Catholic. Unfortunately the British, who took over the French territory following the fall of Quebec, failed to maintain such harmonious relations with the Passamaquoddies. It's a familiar and sad

Old cannery—Eastport

story. The Indians felt they were treated without respect or honor by the arrogant conquerors and very quickly joined Washington's Revolutionary Army. Under Colonel John Allen an eastern Indian outpost was formed at Machias that was largely responsible for keeping Maine in the United States. Generous promises of land and bounty were made to the tribe by the grateful federal government, but when Massachusetts took over local affairs these promises were forgotten, until a treaty was finally agreed to in 1794. Then in 1820 Maine regained its independent status, and although it undertook to accept all prior treaties, devious court decisions and corruption in political circles led to abandonment of most agreements. The Indians were ultimately left to fend for themselves, without financial assistance and without most of their land.

Although recent grants and programs have benefited the Passamaquoddies, there is still resentment in the tribe over the way they were treated. Nevertheless they maintain their independent existence. A considerable portion of their income is derived from local fishing activities, including the use of weirs and seines to catch the herring shoals that run close to the land through Passamaquoddy Bay. The fish, confused by the barrier of vertical nets blocking their path, turn and follow the barrier into a circular net pen, or weir, from which they are scooped up by purse-seine nets into the fishing boats. There are a number of these unusual-looking pens in the bay; photographers often find them excellent subjects, especially when silhouetted against a brilliant sunset.

Three miles across the bay from Eastport (but almost forty miles by road) is another fishing, canning and packing town, Lubec. Its economy also has been unsteady in recent years, although it receives a little more attention from tourists than Eastport due to the proximity of Campobello Island, onetime summer resort of FDR and the Roosevelt family. A graceful bridge links the island to the town, but Americans should remember the island is Canadian territory and be prepared to stop at the customs office.

Campobello is a delightful little world to explore, possessing fine coastal scenery, narrow back roads and the two charming villages of Welshpool and Wilson's Beach. The most popular attraction of course is 2600-acre International Park, which includes the old Roosevelt vacation home and a varied landscape of woods, marshes, beaches and rocky cliffs. The family first began to summer on the estate in 1885. For many years after Franklin had fallen victim to polio, he did not go to the island. Then in 1933, following the first hundred days of his presidential administration, he spent a few relaxing days here; he enjoyed similar periods during the summers of 1936 and 1939. Although his stays were always short he maintained a strong devotion to his "beloved isle" and its inhabitants. Today Canadians on Campobello still refer to him as "our Mr. President."

North Lubec, a part of Lubec Township on Cobscook Bay, was once a copper-mining center, but is perhaps better known as the site of one of New England's few gold "discoveries." The whole affair was a scandalous confidence trick devised by a gentleman named Jernegan, who, as pastor of a nearby parish, convinced faithful followers, and even hard-nosed metropolitan businessmen, that he had developed a machine for extracting gold from seawater. His enterprise, the Electrolytic Marine Salts Company, came into existence in 1896, and within a short time its stock had been sold all over the country and a large plant built. At this point, there's some confusion in the story. We know without doubt that Jernegan "salted" the ocean floor with gold dust to attract rapid investment, but there's also some evidence to suggest he did indeed manage to extract a measure of the precious metal from seawater. Unfortunately we shall never know for sure. After a few months Jernegan vanished with company funds. Those left behind couldn't make the plant function effectively and abandoned it in 1898.

Totem pole—Quoddy

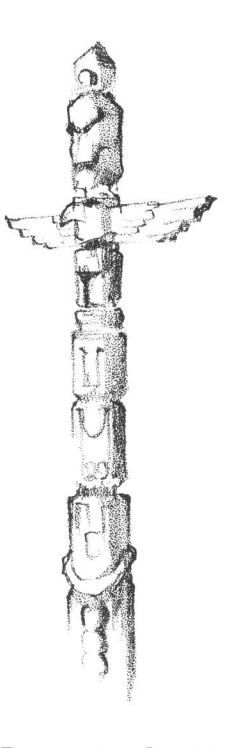

West of the fascinating Moosehorn National Wildlife Refuge, set in typical hunting country along Routes 86 and 191, is the Machias region—another area of Maine's eastern coast full of seafaring history. Although the town was originally founded by the Pilgrims as a fur-trading post in 1633, deep in the heart of what was then French territory, Governor La Tour of Acadia soon chased out the English settlers. The site remained a wilderness for several decades until it became a base for coastal pirates, who were making rapid fortunes by selling stolen goods to a populace tired of being restricted to high-priced English products. In the early 1700s the "Robin Hood of the High Seas," Samuel Bellamy, selected the location for a pirate's utopia, an independent kingdom where pirates could live a life of ease. He forced his scores of captured prisoners to construct an elaborate fort and then set out on what was intended to be a preretirement voyage—an excursion to collect women, wine and valuables before settling down to enjoy his earthly paradise. Unfortunately it turned out to be a disastrous trip for the aging pirate. Not only did he mistakenly attempt to capture a French merchantman laden with troops and hidden cannons—an error that left his ship *Whidaw* severely battered—but he was deceived by the captain of his next prize, a New Bedford whaler. Bellamy always invited a captured crew to join him in his "take from the rich, give to the poor" voyages, and apparently the whaler crew agreed. The captain offered to guide Bellamy through the dangerous reefs of the Massachusetts coast, then purposely ran his own vessel aground and watched as the *Whidaw* was smashed upon the rocks, drowning Bellamy and most of his pirate crew.

So the fort was abandoned and Machias never became an outlaw's utopia. Instead it was the site of the first naval battle of the Revolution in 1775, when local citizens, annoyed at British demands for lumber and by removal of a recently erected Liberty Pole, commandeered a local merchant ship and captured the British vessel *Margaretta*. It was an incredible escapade. An old Indian fighter, Colonel John O'Brien, led his crew of pitchfork-wielding locals against the heavily armed vessel and won the day after killing the British captain and many of his crew. But that was only the beginning. The ambitious colonel, now retitled "captain," sped off and captured two other British ships, so delighting Washington

Commune—near Cutler

that he later made Fort Machias part of the new nation's national defense frontier. The British avoided the town, and it was not until 1814, during the War of 1812, that they captured the fort and held it for a brief period prior to the signing of the peace treaty.

So much for this region's tumultuous history. Today, it's more peaceful than most of Maine's coastal peninsulas yet just as beautiful. Quoddy Head, with its red-striped lighthouse and impressive views across the bay toward the high cliffed island of Grand Manan, is a perfect spot to spend an off-season evening.

And I remember the peace of the people. There is a small colony of young artists living in imaginatively designed "yurts" and, as the sketch shows, a remarkable multisided, three-story tower alongside the Cutler Road. I spent some time here enjoying their company, their simple food and their philosophy. "We live close to ourselves, to our own spirits," one girl told me. "We don't mind people coming here—it's good to see them thinking of alternative ways of living. We love what we do, the things we make, the experiences we share together. It's so full—full of energy, full of love and trust, full of unity. We feel part of everything around us, and best of all, we feel part of one another." She laughed a lovely laugh, waving her hand over a distant vista of bays, inlets and islands. "It's just . . . so incredibly beautiful!"

Lowe's Covered Bridge—near Guilford

26. THE GUILFORD/JACKMAN LOOP
On the Edge of the Allagash

Recent improvement of the roads, coupled with the increasing popularity of the Allagash/Katahdin region to the north and east of Greenville, has removed some of this area's "hidden" flavor. Nevertheless it remains, in comparison with the often overcrowded coastal resorts, a relatively quiet but dramatic portion of Maine's northern wilderness—and well worth exploration.

The rectangular loop route begins at Lowe's Covered Bridge, a couple of miles west of Dover-Foxcroft on Route 15, and passes through the once "utopian" community of Guilford. The original settlers of this small woolen-mill town were determined to control the quality of the population intake. They agreed upon a covenant to admit "no person as a settler who is not industrious, orderly, moral and well disposed." Little did they realize in those early days that the area was destined to become one of New England's most active lumbering areas, a region renowned for burly jacks whose appetites and vocabularies would be legendary.

Tiny Abbott Village also once possessed a number of thriving mills (the sketch shows all that remains). Take Route 16 to the left, just by the local store, and follow it through the forest-covered hills to Bingham. It's a beautiful drive, especially in the fall season when, for mile after winding mile, travelers experience a continuous sequence of blazing colors interspersed with panoramas of the Bald Mountain area to the north and the rolling, lake-dotted country to the south.

Along one quiet stretch of this drive I found a roadside cemetery almost hidden by trees and bushes. A few of the headstones were rich purple slate from the nearby mines near Monson. As with many rural burial grounds, the stories of lost lives are told with sad brevity:

> THREE INFANTS
> CHILDREN OF
> THOMAS D. AND SUSAN B.
> TITCOMB
> INTERRED
> MARCH 2, 1851.

Remnants of a mill—Abbott Village

The long descent into the Kennebec Valley at Bingham is spectacular as range after range of hills and mountains appears in the distance. The view is always changing as the road twists and curves, the majesty of the scene always framed by birches and maples.

At the base of the descent the drive northward along the Kennebec River begins. This must be one of New England's most beautiful journeys. The river is enclosed all the way to West Forks in a deep wooded valley, and flows fast and sparkling in the narrow sections. Occasionally it widens, as at the Wyman Dam. A mile or two upstream from the retaining wall I caught a glimpse of a vast logpile held in place by a curved chain boom. The logs, literally scores of thousands all packed together in a kind of random herringbone pattern, are held in this way on the water until clearance is given them to be floated over the wall and sluiced downstream to the mills. The pile I saw must have been one of the last, for recent court decisions have forbidden log driving on the rivers of Maine, thus terminating the romantic era of the river rider and "the days of the long log." The area is still full of stories of the time when lumberjacks would ride the great gray snakes of logs downstream, across rapids, over falls, through the gorges, with long-handled peaveys, pickpoles and, of course, dynamite to break the inevitable jams. They traveled light: "A tin cup, plate, knife and spoon were adequate. Very few white-water drives boasted forks; any man dumb enough to ask the cook for a fork was labelled a 'deadwater' or 'greenhorn' by his companions."

Clothes were also considered unimportant and rarely required changing, as the loggers invariably took plenty of impromptu baths in these churning streams during the spring drive. However, boots were another matter. From all accounts, these were one of the few extravagances drivers allowed themselves while on the job, but they were also wise insurance. A sound pair of calked boots, permitting nimble movement on the racing logs, could often mean the difference between a safe drive and a grisly death under tons of churning lumber. A few weeks prior to the drive the camps were filled with lumberjacks breaking in their new custom-made boots.

These spring drives brought life and vigor to the communities along the logging rivers—the Allagash, the St. John, the St. Regis, the Machias and the Kennebec. It was almost like a traveling carnival. The company advance men came first, checking the river for ice jams; then the chuck wagon ("wangun") raced ahead to an agreed-upon nighttime rendezvous downstream; then the logs and their drivers proceeded, followed sometimes by a second cook shack (for snacks), often on a log raft. Finally came the doctors and nurses, important company officials in fancy carriages and all the hangers-on—the peddlers, logger-style "groupies," acrobats, jugglers, liquor salesmen, fortune tellers, even the occasional mobile bordello for late-night recreation. Mothers kept their daughters carefully locked up when the jacks came through, but tavernkeepers and storeowners, particularly at the end-of-drive towns, often made overnight fortunes from the free-spending, whiskey-drinking, good-time-seeking men of the forest. It was then that raucous lumbering songs filled a dozen or more nights of frantic indulgence:

Main street—Caratunk

'Tis when we do go into the woods—
Drink round, brave boys! Drink round, brave boys!
'Tis when we do go into the woods,
Jolly brave boys are we.

This refrain would be followed by thirty or forty verses describing all the intricacies of the lumbering business.

Farther up the Kennebec Valley, Route 201 crosses the old Arnold Trail. Here a series of displays tell the sad saga of Benedict Arnold's attempt to lead an army of 1100 men up the Kennebec and Dead River Valleys to capture the British-held city of Quebec in the winter of 1775–76. Not only was the expedition a dismal failure, but the sequence of spirit-breaking events that occurred during the long haul northward makes one marvel that Arnold and his depleted company ever reached Quebec at all. It's worth pausing here at the trail to read the full story. Benedict Arnold is commonly regarded as an infamous Revolutionary traitor, and such brave escapades as this ill-fated attack are generally overlooked or forgotten.

Just north of the Arnold Trail marker the road passes over the Appalachian Trail at Caratunk. The village itself, set back from the main highway, is a fine example of a mountain community, with its white clapboard cottages and general store slumbering along a quiet street. It's a brief but lovely detour.

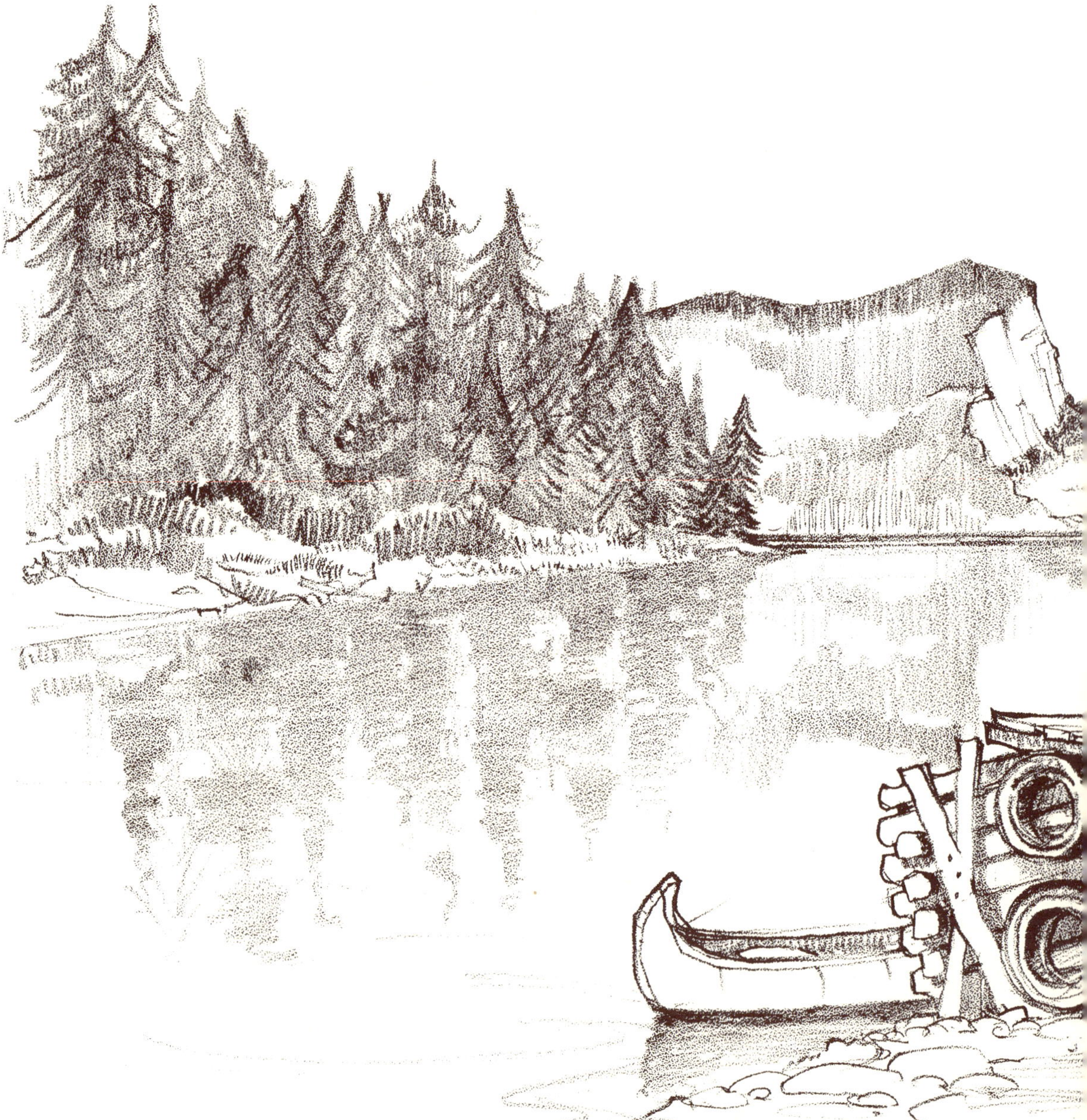

Moosehead Lake and Mount Kineo

Route 201 leaves the Kennebec at West Forks and climbs northward through dark fir forests. The vistas, although frustratingly brief, are broader; wide valleys and strongly profiled mountains recede in blue and purple haze. The old lumbering town of Jackman is an excellent base for exploring this region around the Canadian border, and there's a fine resort, the Sky Lodge, on the hillside north of the town. French influence is quite marked. The Roman Catholic church, next door to Jackman's Marie-Joseph Hospital, has all the sturdy construction and rich detailing of those found to the north in the province of Quebec. Even the store signs are occasionally bilingual—such as one for the Till Midnight Store, which, literally translated, becomes Jusqu'à Minuit Magasin!

From Jackman travel eastward on Route 15, past Long Pond and the strange, dead-tree-littered shores of Brassua Lake (a driftwood collector's paradise). At the resort town of Rockwood the road turns southward, with good views of Moosehead Lake, Mount Kineo and, way in the distance, the Katahdin peaks. For the true traveler, explorer or hunter, Rockwood and the nearby town of Greenville are starting points for journeys into the great wilderness of Baxter State Park and the Allagash region. Many of the roads are private, some requiring fees, but if you have a sturdy car and a yen for some unforgettable back country travel, past spectacular lakes and mountains with ancient Indian names, then this is where it all begins. Canoe enthusiasts know the area well—the Allagash Wilderness Waterway is perhaps the most famous of all of Maine's canoe trips. Although considerable portage and whitewater travel is necessary, the silent beauty of the forest-bordered lakes is, I am told, without equal in the eastern United States.

The drive southward from Greenville is a series of long descents from high mountain and fir country to the lower deciduous land around Dover-Foxcroft and the Piscataquis Valley. En route there are a few interesting side trips, particularly around Monson, where bumpy back roads lead to such frontier-style towns as Blanchard and Shirley Mills. The latter was the birthplace of one of America's best humorists, Edgar Wilson (Bill) Nye, who once described his home community as situated "amid the barren and inhospitable waste of rocks and cold—the last place in the world that a great man would select to be born"! Actually it's a charming little community, situated by a small pond and apparently unchanged since the writer's birth in 1850. It's rarely visited by outsiders, possibly because there are few if any directional signs on the main road.

A final side trip, before reaching the comparative urbanity of Dover-Foxcroft, is a visit to Sebec Lake. On the town side there's a small state park, but I prefer the quieter drive from the North Guilford Road to the lake's pastoral western shore.

Although I have spent much time exploring this wilderness country, the more I read of great canoe trips on Moosehead Lake, the Kennebec and the Allagash, the more I realize that until I launch myself on one of those tumbling waterways I have only just begun to discover the true beauty and richness of this region.

Sunken potato barn

27. HOULTON AND VICINITY
Where the Potato Is King

I have never found potatoes particularly interesting. There's something about their amorphous shape and dull, gray-brown color that fails to impress my aesthetic sensibilities. I have become used to the scrubbed and polished pyramids in supermarkets, elaborately printed plastic bags displaying rounded bulges and those mushy, foil-wrapped versions, often served in a forest of parsley sprigs, at fancy restaurants. But in common with many of my overweight colleagues I chose to eliminate the potato from my diet, and over the past two or three years, with the exception of an occasional indulgence in french fries, have virtually ignored its existence.

However, this was all prior to my visit to Aroostook County in northern Maine, one of the largest potato-growing areas in the country. In the days spent exploring this area, talking to the farmers and eating at local restaurants, my enthusiasm for this most misunderstood of all domestic vegetables returned. I am now again an admirer of the versatility of these humble gray "apples of the earth" and am considered by many of my new-found colleagues (the old bunch seemed to consider me a deserter from their cause) to be something of a gourmet cook when it comes to the preparation of potato dishes. Unfortunately space does not allow for the inclusion of actual recipes, but you might get some ideas for unusual concoctions if you talk to some of the residents of Aroostook.

Travelers, however, should be warned that this is no tourist area. The rolling, open hills, stretching away almost as far as the eye can see, are in marked contrast to the conifer-covered headlands, rocky inlets and lobster villages of the coast, or the forest and lake areas to the west in the Allagash/Katahdin region. The potato-growing part of Aroostook is hard-working country. The people, many of French origin (see "The St. John Valley"—page 169), have a bronzed and weathered look. It is a land of climatic extremes—hot summers, driving winds and rains in late autumn, long, frozen winter months when the snow blasts across the fields in great whirling eddies, drifting against the high barns and hedgerows. Yet on a warm evening or early summer morning, when the tiny white potato blossoms glitter in endless green rows, the landscape has beauty—a sense of wide, fresh space similar to that of the wheat plains of Nebraska and Kansas.

It is a unique area, almost half the size of Connecticut, with colorful communities, plain-spoken, open people and always, dominating everywhere you look, King Potato. Old, wheezing trucks bounce through the fields or down the rutted back roads laden with potatoes in large gray barrels. In the fall potato pickers by the thousands flock in from adjoining states and Canada for the frantic September harvest. Even the schools close down for the period to allow the kids to join in the picking. And what a sight that is—reminiscent of those early Van Gogh sketches of potato pickers in Holland. Groups of bent figures with colorful hats and jackets move together slowly among the furrows, picking, plucking, stamping, then bending and stretching again to fill the next barrel. "It's killing. God knows why I do it," a middle-aged lady from Houlton told me during a break for the midday sandwich. Apparently her whole family was in the field with her. "It gets lonely if you stay at home. Everyone's out here making money—all mine are here, sixteen, I think—but will I be glad when it's over. My back's never got used to this bending. Some work on their knees, y'know—that's even worse." From what I could learn,

"Continuous architecture"

Barns—near Knowles Corner

the pay rate per barrel picked is generally good. Many families rely upon the harvest to supplement an otherwise inadequate annual income.

The area around Houlton and the adjoining villages of Ludlow, Smyrna Mills, Littleton and Knowles Corner contains some particularly interesting examples of potatoland architecture. Note the unusual barn almost submerged in the soil as a way to maintain even temperature and humidity for stored potatoes. These are a familiar sight throughout eastern Aroostook and the rolling hills around Presque Isle, Fort Fairfield and Caribou to the north.

Another common vernacular is the stringing together of farmhouse, outhouses, sheds and even the main barn in a continuum of space. All are linked together so that even during the worst months of winter farmers may attend to the necessary tasks, machine maintenance and regular storage inspection without setting foot outside. The sketch shows one of my favorite examples of "continuous architecture," sitting on top of a high, open field overlooking the endless undulating and furrowed landscape.

On the western fringe of the potato area along Route 11 near Knowles Corner, dairy farming begins to predominate. Gone are the half-submerged barns; in their place are tall, sturdy structures, some lonely and dilapidated, like the magnificent specimens on page 163, others forming part of bold yet sensitive groupings of farm buildings. I found one complex, the Townsend Farm, by the roadside near Knowles Corner. The land behind the buildings slopes gently down to the forest, and in the far distance, almost fifty miles away, rises the great mass of Katahdin and its peers. The view was incredibly beautiful. It happened to be a perfect evening, but in any kind of weather, at any time of day, one could not fail to be impressed by such a sight.

For those looking to enjoy more intimate contact with the great mountain, there's a road leading directly to Baxter State Park from the town of Patten, a short distance to the west. Alternatively, if a true rough-country adventure is sought, try the private lumber road from Ashland, farther to the north, through eighty miles of magnificent forest into Baxter and then exit via Patten or Millinocket farther south. If you take either of these journeys you will receive warnings galore from the lumber companies and the state park authorities about the condition of roads, the dangers of wilderness driving, and so forth. All I can add from firsthand experience is: be ready to spend some money on the trip (there are charges for park entry, camping and use of private roads) and take a car that can stand a considerable amount of rough riding, especially if you select the Ashland route.

Views of Katahdin are not the only memorable vistas in the Houlton area. To the south of Houlton itself Route 1 passes along a high ridge overlooking the vast expanses of Grand Lake. There are few scenes in northern New England to match the majesty of these great sweeps of water interlaced with fingers of thick forest.

On a more intimate scale, there are some lovely scenes along the back roads in the Limerick/Oakfield area, particularly on the one that passes Pleasant Pond and meanders eastward through wooded hills to Linneus. It was along here that I found a most unusual little cemetery at the side of the road. There were no stone markers at all—just simple white wooden crosses with hand-painted names and nineteenth-century burial dates. I chatted with an old man in one of those baseball-type hats (the traditional headgear of Maine males) who was passing in a battered truck. "Oh, these was poor folk down this way. Couldn't afford no proper stones—many of 'em are still buried back there in the woods, where they lived. Someone cleaned up this burial ground, but them's only a few that lived around these parts." I looked at the scrub and forest that grew to the very edges of the dusty track and realized how quickly the signs of man's existence in the area had been eliminated. All that remained was a few segments of stone wall and an occasional apple tree that obviously was once part of a garden or small holding.

Townsend Farm—near Knowles Corner

Houlton is a marked contrast to its potato field and forest hinterland. It's a bustling county town full of fine public buildings and possessing a generous selection of old mansions along the Meduxnekeag River. The market square is invariably the active center of the town, full of traffic and noise during the day. Although Houlton has lost some of its importance as the potato capital of the region (the title is more aptly bestowed on Presque Isle), it has developed as a nucleus for other crops, most notably sugar beets, timber and fern fiddleheads. The last-mentioned delicacies, still available only at exclusive restaurants, are harvested in May along the river banks; they make delicious eating, especially with some of Aroostook's gourmet potato dishes.

There is much of interest in this region. For the history-minded there are museums at Houlton and, farther to the north, at Van Buren, New Sweden and St. David (see "The St. John Valley"—page 171). For camera enthusiasts there are the forests and great vistas to the west around Katahdin; and for lovers of the unusual there is the rolling landscape itself with its friendly people and fascinating architecture. It's an area that should not be missed.

Potato barrel mailbox

28. THE ST. JOHN VALLEY
The Acadian Land of Evangeline

> This is the forest primeval; but where are the hearts that beneath it
> Leapt like the roe, when he hears in the woodland the voice of the
>   huntsman?
> Where is the thatched-roofed village, the home of Acadian farmers,
> Men whose lives glided on like rivers that water the woodlands,
> Darkened by shadows of earth, but reflecting an image of heaven?
> Waste are those pleasant farms, and the farmers forever departed!

So begins Longfellow's somber poem "Evangeline: A Tale of Acadie," which tells, through the guise of two parted lovers, the story of the Acadian migrations during the late 1700s. It's a story of a broken race, a culture almost destroyed by constant eviction from its homelands in Canada and northern Maine. It's a tragic record of divided families and lost love's. When, after a lifetime of searching, Evangeline finds the love of her youth, Gabriel, in a hospital, he dies in her arms whispering her name with his last breath.

The legend, supposedly based on a true occurrence, is still very real to the remaining members of this blond-haired race from France's Brittany and Normandy. Many of them live today in Madawaska, a region encompassing territory in both Maine and New Brunswick, Canada, and centered along the upper St. John River Valley between Fort Kent and Fort Fairfield.

But these people are only the fortunate few. Remnants of the Acadian people have been scattered literally throughout the Western world since they were exiled by the British in 1755 from their original homeland of Nova Scotia. From the point of view of George II of England, these Frenchmen living in recently conquered territory were a threat to the security of the area, particularly as they steadfastly refused to take an oath requiring them to join with British forces against any future French attacks. There was a fear that if such an attack came the Acadians might instead turn on the Crown. So, in an event known as "Le Grand Dérangement," almost the entire population was arbitrarily subdivided into small groups and dispatched by ship to other colonies on the East Coast and even to France, England, the West Indies, Bermuda and Corsica.

For years these poor people wandered from region to region, country to country. Many settled in the bayous of Louisiana, which was still in French hands (hence today's "Cajuns"), but most of the others lived in hostile territory, unwelcome and unfamiliar with the language, customs and religion.

Following the Treaty of Paris in 1763, when Britain became mistress over all Canada, many of the Acadians came home. No longer considered dangerous, as the French influence had been destroyed, they were allowed to settle around Fredericton, New Brunswick. But only a few years later they were dispersed again—this time by Tory loyalists from New England, who found themselves unpopular in America following the Revolution. The Tories rejected them as "French squatters" and took over their lands and possessions, forcing the Acadians in 1785 to move even farther northward up the St. John River into what is now the Madawaska region. A cross in the field below the church at St. David marks the spot of their original landing.

But although Britain approved the move and offered a land grant of two hundred acres to every Acadian family, their troubles were not over. In fact they found themselves trapped again between two nationalities—this time the British and the Americans—just as they had been several decades earlier during the British and French Wars. The land on which they had been encouraged to settle was not legally in British hands but rather part of a disputed boundary area. In the early 1800s there was talk of making the contested region an independent nation, but the land-hungry authorities on both sides soon rejected that proposal. Frantic colonization of the St. John Valley was engaged in by both Britain and the United States; forts were built along the river, and structures such as the sturdy blockhouse at Fort Kent (page 172), completed in 1840, once formed part of the defenses for the ten thousand American troops stationed here. The bloodless and often forgotten Aroostook War, which almost brought the two nations into a third major conflict, was merely one of the many crises during this turbulent era. Finally, in 1842, Lord Ashburton and Daniel Webster hammered out an agreement that

Church and cross—St. David

satisfied no one but at least ended the disputes. The Acadians, of course, came off the worst. The Canadian/American boundary line was drawn along the center of the St. John River, neatly bisecting their third and final homeland. But by that time in their history the Acadians could accept almost any event with a stoicism that came from years of continual disaster.

At least they have managed to retain their region, and many, particularly the "true stock" in the village of St. David, are actively involved in nurturing their old culture, language and lifestyle. There's a small but interesting museum here, just by the church, containing many of the old Acadian domestic utensils and agricultural implements. The spinning wheels and large wooden loom are authentic, and there's talk of reviving the old art of blanket and carpet weaving in the locality. Another, similar museum can be found farther down the road in Van Buren. Both are expressions of a new pride, a new consciousness of heritage. The Acadians still weep at the story of Evangeline, but now at last they have a permanent home along this beautiful river.

And the valley is extraordinarily beautiful, particularly the stretch from Fort Kent to the town of Madawaska. Lower down, in the St. David/Van Buren area, the artifacts of civilization intrude a little more blatantly. Garish bilingual signs (most of this region of Maine is still French-speaking) denote roadside motels. A miscellany of tasteless "Québec Mo-

Blockhouse at Fort Kent

derne" homes contrasts sharply with the older, New England-style cottages. There are raised doorways on many of the homes, an indication of long, snowbound winters. Extravagant Baroque churches, their domes and spires painted with chrome alum, can be found along Route 1 north of Van Buren, and narrow strip fields flow down the valley sides into swampy patches along the river. It truly feels like a frontier land—an often brash, lively place, very different from the neat, typical New England landscape of southern Maine with its crisp architecture and carefully nurtured greens. Yet some of the villages, particularly those on the Canadian side, possess an almost southern European character, their tightly clustered homes huddled around the dominant profile of a Roman Catholic church with tall, silvered spires.

Just above the valley, up over the steep ridges, there's a landscape of unusual beauty and variety. The Van Buren–Caribou road (Route 1) passes first through an area of open, rolling potato fields, the staple crop of Aroostook (see "Houlton and Vicinity"—page 163). Then, after a few miles, the scenery changes to thick pine and birch woods, a reminder of the days when the St. John Valley was a major lumbering center. Now much of the growth is secondary or even tertiary, and the major lumbering operations have moved westward to the endless forests of the Allagash/Katahdin region—although large paper mills still exist in Madawaska.

Somewhere along this route I sketched a village store. I had been inside briefly to buy some supplies, and came away shocked at the apparent poverty of the inhabitants round about. The shelves, randomly fixed to cracked plaster walls, were just barely stocked with essential staples—flour, bread, beans, sugar and canned meat. There were loose sacks of potatoes on the floor, a few bottles of soda and an old refrigerator filled with cartons of beer. It was a cold day and there was no heat in the store's barn-like interior. The only customer stamped his feet on the concrete floor, and the girl behind the counter wore two gray scarves and mittens as she totaled the grocery bill on a tiny scratchpad. The only lighting was two forty-watt bulbs dangling from the ceiling on long wires.

To the west along Route 161 I heard some sad stories about the decline of the region. I was visiting the old Swedish colony centered around the villages of Stockholm, Jemtland, Sweden and New Sweden, and found

Church—Lille

A village store in potato country

myself chatting with a middle-aged gas station owner who had blue eyes and blond hair—the appropriate Scandinavian features. " 'Course I've not been here as long as some of 'em—the Svensons, the Carlstroms, the Andersons—place is full of Andersons—but I remember when this was a real lively area. Stockholm, have you seen it? Tiny place now, few houses, a church. Why, that place had factories all down the valley. A big veneer works too—logs used to go right through the town on the Little Madawaska. There was a railroad station too. Lots of noise, lots of people, lots of money!"

As I strolled down Stockholm's quiet main street, I found it hard to imagine that this had been such a bustling community around the turn of the century. It seemed lost in the forest, almost as it must have been when the little colony of fifty Swedes arrived in 1870. They were brought over by the United States consul to Sweden, William Widgery Thomas, Jr., wooed with promises of free land, new cabins and even cook stoves. Unfortunately there was some confusion of intent, for when the hardy immigrants arrived after a long westward trek from Halifax, Nova Scotia, they found that very little had been prepared for them. Those who remained were obliged to fend for themselves in a wild land of unexplored virgin forest. This kind of "misunderstanding" was quite familiar in Maine—a similar event occurred at Waldoboro with a group of German immigrants (see "The Bristol Peninsula"—page 130).

A charming middle-aged schoolteacher who lives in a large Victorian house overlooking the main street told me that for all the economic problems of the region during the past few decades, the small villages still retain their Swedish spirit and culture, though mingled somewhat with Acadian influences. There are three main festivals in the year: Lucia, a derivation of the pagan Festival of Lights, held in mid-December; the Mid-Summer Festival in Thomas Park at New Sweden, featuring maypole dancing, and on July 23 a celebration commemorating the arrival of the first Swedish colonists.

With the exception of an interestingly detailed Baptist church at New Sweden, there is little Scandinavian-flavored architecture in the area. However, the small museum in the same village provides some fascinating insights of life during the early days of this unusual colony.

There's one last part of this region I love: up on the undulating plateau between Route 161 and the St. John River. I found it almost by accident one day while trying to locate a short cross-country route to Madawaska from the west. It's an area of fields and woods distinguished by the appropriately named Long Lake. There are some weekend cottages along the shore, but generally it's undeveloped. On a windy day the waves whip down the lake in lines of white crests, crashing like the sea on the sandy shores. But on a calm day, especially around dawn, the lake is often perfectly still, mirroring the gentle landscape and the groups of trees along its edge. It's the kind of place you want to come back to; it stays in your memory for a long time. The Acadians love it too, and must find peace here, a rest from their recollections of stolen homelands, divided families and lost loves.

Index

Abbott Village, Me., 156, 157
Acadians, 169-171, 175
Adams, Clarence, 58-59
Adams, George Washington, 146-147
Addison, Me., 147
Albany, Vt., 111
Alexandria, N.H., 88
Algonkian Indians, 85, 151
Allagash River Valley, 156, 158, 162
Allen, Ethan, 9, 16, 18
Allen, Colonel John, 152
Allen House (Cuttyhunk Island), 41
Alna, Me., 135
Alton, R.I., 39
Amherst, Mass., 24
Androscoggin River, 114, 127
Appalachian Gap, 97
Appalachian Trail, 159

Archer, Gabriel, 44
Arnold, Benedict, 112, 159
Arnold Trail, 159
Aroostook County, Me., 148, 163-168
Aroostook War, 170
Ash Point, Me., 141, 142
Avalon Club, 45

Back Lake, 125
Baldface, Mount, 88
Ball, Albert, 71
Balsams Resort, 127
Barber, Father Virgil, 73
Barnard, F. A. P., 31
Barre, Vt., 102
Baxter State Park, Me., 162, 166
Baynes, Ernest Harold, 83-84
Beals Island, 145, 147

Beede, Daniel, 91
Beede Falls, 92-93
Bellamy, Samuel, 153-154
Bellows, Colonel Benjamin, 57
Bellows Falls, Vt., 54-57
Bentley, W. A., 102
Berkshire Hills, 29, 30-35, 49
Berlin, N.H., 127
Bicknell, Chandler Clarence, 35
Bingham, Me., 156-157, 158
Blanchard, Me., 162
Bloody Brook Massacre, 28
Blueberry Barrens, 143-144
Blue Mountain Forest Reservation, 83-84
Boullard, Isaac, 66
Bow, N.H., 67-69
Bradford, N.H., 64-65, 66-67
Bradford, R.I., 39
Braintree, Vt., 95
Brandon, Vt., 95
Brassua Lake, 162
Brattleboro, Vt., 54
Bread Loaf, Vt., 96
Bristol, Me., 134, 135
Bristol, R.I., 38
Bristol, Vt., 95-96, 99
Bristol Mills, Me., 135
Bristol Peninsula, 130-135
Brown, John, 133
Brush, George de Forest, 50
Bryant, William Cullen, 30-31, 35
Buckland, Mass., 35
Bull, Dixey, 133
Bunker Hill, Me., 135

Cabot, John, 138
Cabot, Vt., 102-103
Cabot, Mount, 115
Calais, Me., 151
Calais, Vt., 102, 103-104
Campobello Island, 153
Campton, N.H., 91
Canaan, N.H., 85-87
Canaan, Vt., 123, 125
Canaan Center, N.H., 85-86, 88
Caratunk, Me., 159
Cardigan, Mount, 88
Cardigan State Park, N.H., 88
Caribou, Me., 165, 168, 172
Caspian Lake, 111
Castin, Baron de, 133
Cathedral Pines, 17
Cathedral Woods, 141
Cedar Pond, 115
Center Sandwich, N.H., 91, 92, 93, 94

Champlain, Lake, 97, 99
Champlain, Samuel de, 131, 138, 151
Charlestown, R.I., 37, 38
Chase, Philander, 83
Chase, Wareham, 103
Chester, Vt., 58-59, 60, 61
Chesterfield Gorge, 35
Christine Lake, 114-115
Churaevka, Conn., 13
Churchill, Winston (novelist), 80
Church of Christ, Scientist, 67-69
Claremont, N.H., 70-73
Clarendon Springs, Vt., 74-75
Cobscook Bay, 153
Cockermouth River, 85
Colburn, Zerah, 102-103
Colebrook, N.H., 125-126
Colrain, Mass., 33
Coniston (Churchill), 80
Connecticut, 8-19
Connecticut River, 24, 54, 56, 95, 117, 125, 126
Connecticut Valley, 29, 35, 80, 83
Conway, N.H., 94
Cooper's Mill, Me., 135
Coos County, N.H., 122
Corbin, Austin, 83
Coreser, Simeon, 95-96
Cornish Bridge, 83
Cornish Mills, Vt., 83
Cornish region, Vt., 80-84
Cornwall, Conn., 14-19
Cothren, William, 9-10
Craftsbury Academy, 108
Craftsbury Common, Vt., 108-109, 111
Crocker, Reverend Henry, 102
Cummington, Mass., 30-32
Cutler, Me., 149, 154-155
Cuttyhunk Island, 40-45

Damariscotta, Me., 130
Damariscotta Lake, 135
Dead River Valley, 159
Deblois, Me., 143, 148
Deerfield, Mass., 28-29
Devil's Slide, 116
Dixville Notch, 126, 127
Dorrelites, 66
Dover-Foxcroft, Me., 156, 162
Dublin, N.H., 49-50
Durgin Bridge, 94

East Burke, Vt., 121
East Calais, Vt., 104, 107
East Craftsbury, Vt., 113
Eastport, Me., 149-151, 152

178

East Poultney, Vt., 77-78, 79
East Washington, N.H., 65
Eddy, Mary Baker, 67-69
Elizabeth Islands, 40, 41
Ellis River Valley, 94
Emerson, Ralph Waldo, 50, 61
Errol, N.H., 127
Ethan Allen, Mount, 97
"Evangeline" (Longfellow), 169, 171

Fernside (Shaker community), 21
Field, Captain Earl, 136-137, 139
Field, Eugene, 62
Finnegan, Father Patrick J., 73
First Connecticut Lake, 125
Fort Fairfield, Me., 165, 169
Fort Kent, Me., 169, 170, 171, 172
Fort William Henry, 131-133
Foster, Joseph, 52
Fowler, Orson, 110
Frances, Lake, 125
Franklin, N.H., 85, 87
Frost, Robert, 96

Gallup Mills, Vt., 120
Gibson, William Hamilton, 11
Glastonbury, Conn., 119
Gold, Martin, 14-15
Goose Pond, 88-89
Goshen, Conn., 14
Gosnold, Bartholomew, 44-45, 138
Gospel Hollow, Vt., 104, 105
Grafton, Vt., 61
Granby, Vt., 120-121
Grand Lake, 167
Grand Manan Island, 155
Grassroots Project, 108
Graves, Isaac and John, 25
Great Rhode Island Swamp, 36-39
Greeley, Horace, 77-78
Green, Henrietta Howland Robinson, 57
Greenfield, Mass., 29, 33
Greenfield River, 33
Green Mountains, 54-63, 74-78, 95-101
Greensboro, Vt., 111-113
Greensboro Bend, Vt., 121
Greenville, Me., 156, 162
Griswold, John, 17
Groveton, N.H., 117
Guildhall, Vt., 117-119
Guilford, Me., 156
Gunn, Frederick W., 11

Hadley, Mass., 28, 29
Hale, Edward Everett, 28
Hale, Henry, 127

Hall, Matthew, 61
Hall, Moses, 91-92
Hallock, Homan, 32-33
Hancock, Mass., 110
Hancock, N.H., 53
Happy Hollow, N.H., 122, 125
Hardwick, Vt., 66-67
Harris, Milan, 52
Harrisville, N.H., 50-52, 53
Hatfield, Mass., 24-29
Hawthorne, Nathaniel, 50
Hazen, General Moses, 113
Hazen's Notch, Vt., 112
Head Tide, Me., 135
Hebron, N.H., 85
Hell's Half Acre, 95-96
Hill, N.H., 87-88
Hinsdale, Mass., 32
Hitchcock, Alfred, 111
Holiday in the Hills Fair, 120
Hoosac Tunnel, 34, 35
Hopkins, Mark, 31
Horeb, Mount, 21
Houlton, Me., 163-168
Housatonic Valley, 31-32
Huntingdon Center, Vt., 98
Huntington, Mass., 32, 35

Indian Stream Republic, 122-127
International Park (Campobello Island), 153
Irasburg, Vt., 107, 109-110
Irving, Washington, 89

Jackman, Me., 162
James, Alexander, 50
Janes, Pardon, 103
Jarvis, William, 70
Jefferson, Me., 135
Jemtland, Me., 173
Jericho, Vt., 102
Jerusalem, Vt., 97
Johns, James, 98
Jones, George, 77
Jonesport, Me., 143-148

Kancamagus Highway, 93
Katahdin Mountain, 162, 165, 168
Keene, N.H., 52-53
Kennebec River Valley, 158, 159, 162
Kent, Conn., 18
Kent, Rockwell, 139
Kents' Corner, Vt., 104-105, 106
Kenyon, R.I., 39
Kesar Lake, 64
Kidd, Captain, 95

Kilburn, Mount, 55
Kimball Union Academy, 83
Kineo, Mount, 160-161, 162
King Philip's War, 25-28, 36-38
Kingston, R.I., 37, 38, 39
Kipling, Rudyard, 50, 61
Kitson, Sir Henry, 22-23
Knowles Corner, Me., 165, 166-167
Kosciusko Society, 73

Lambert, Conrad, 72
La Salette Seminary, 87
Lebanon, N.H., 66
Lee, Ann, 21, 22-23
Lee, Mass., 21
Lenox, Mass., 21, 31
Lescarbot, Marc, 151
Lexington, Mass., 22
Lille, Me., 173
Limerick, Me., 167
Lincoln, General Benjamin, 25
Lincoln, N.H., 94
Lincoln, Vt., 96, 99
Linneus, Me., 167
Litchfield, Conn., 8, 9, 14, 17, 18
Littleton, Me., 165
Long Cove, Me., 141
Longfellow, Henry Wadsworth, 169
Long Lake, 175
Long Trail, 99
Loon Lodge and Resort, 94
Loud's Island, 134
Louie's on the Wharf Restaurant, 40
Lowell, Vt., 112
Lower Cabot, Vt., 104
Lowe's Covered Bridge, 156
Lubec, Me., 143, 153
Ludlow, Me., 165
Ludlow, Vt., 95
Lund, Maude, 120-121
Lyme, N.H., 88-89
Lyndon, Vt., 121
Lyon, Mary, 35
Lyon, Colonel Mathew, 15-16

MacDowell Colony, 50, 80
Macedonia State Park, Conn., 18
Machias, Me., 152, 153-155
Machias River, 158
MacKaye, Percy, 84
Madawaska, Me., 169, 170, 171, 173
Maine, 130-175
Manana Island, 137, 138, 139
Maple Corner, Vt., 104
Maple Syrup Museum, 122
Marshall, John, 9-10

Mascoma Lake, 66, 86-87
Massachusetts, 20-35
Mathey, Dean, 61
Mayflower Inn, 11
Meduxnekeag River, 168
Meriden, Vt., 83-84
Metacom, *see* Philip, King
Metallak (Indian woodsman), 125
Micmac Indians, 148
Middlebury College, 96
Middlefield, Mass., 32
Middletown Springs, Vt., 75-76, 77
Milan, N.H., 114-115
Milan Hill, N.H., 115
Miller, William, 107
Millinocket, Me., 166
Mill River, Mass., 21
Milton, Conn., 14, 17-18
Mohawk River, 125
Mohawk Trail, 33-35
"Monadnoc" (Emerson), 50
Monadnock, Mount, 48-50, 126
Monhegan Island, 131, 133, 136-142
Montgomery, Richard, 112
Montpelier, Vt., 98, 102, 104
Moosehead Lake, 160-162
Moosehorn National Wildlife Refuge, 153
Moose River Valley, 121
Moultonborough, N.H., 94
Mud River Valley, 97, 99
Muscongus Bay, 134

Narragansett Indians, 36-38, 39
Nashawena Island, 42
Nelson, N.H., 52, 53
New Bedford, Mass., 40
Newfane, Vt., 62, 63
Newfound Lake, 85, 88
New Hampshire, 48-53, 64-73, 91-94, 114-117, 122-127
New Hampshire League of Arts and Crafts, 93
New Harbor, Me., 132, 133, 138
New Lights, 21, 66-67
New Marlboro, Mass., 21
New Sweden, Me., 168, 173, 175
Newtown, Conn., 8
Niclas, Yolla, 139
North Adams, Mass., 33
Northampton, Mass., 29
North Calais, Vt., 102, 104
North Concord, Vt., 121
Northfield, Mass., 95
North River Valley, 33
North Sandwich, N.H., 94

North Sutton, N.H., 64-65
Norway Pond, 53
Notch road, 90-93
Noyes, John Humphrey, 67
Nye, Edgar Wilson, 162

Oakfield, Me., 167
Obookiah, Henry, 15
O'Brien, Colonel John, 154-155
Old Homestead Museum, 142
Old Tavern (Grafton), 61
Oneida Community, 67
Orange, N.H., 88
Orford, N.H., 89
Orleans County, Vt., 108-113
Osceola, Mount, 91

Parker, Luther, 123
Parrish, Maxfield, 80
Passamaquoddy Bay, 151, 152
Passamaquoddy Indians, 151-152
Passumpsic Valley, 121
Pastoral Days (Gibson), 11
Peacham, Vt., 102, 112
Pemaquid Point, 130, 131-133, 135
Percy, N.H., 115-116
Percy Peaks, 115, 117, 121
Peru, Mass., 32
Peterborough, Vt., 80
Philip, King (Indian leader), 25, 36-38, 133
Phillips, Ray, 139
Phips, Sir William, 133
Pilgrims (Boullard sect), 66
Pioneer Valley, 24-29
Piscataquis Valley, 162
Pittsburg, N.H., 122-125
Plainfield, Mass., 32-33
Plainfield, Vt., 80-82
Pleasant Lake, 167
Pleasant Point Reservation, 151
Pocumtuc Indians, 25
Pomperaug River, 8-9
Port Clyde, Me., 136, 137, 141
Poultney, Vt., 77
Presque Isle, Me., 165, 168
Putney, Vt., 67

Queen Anne's War, 28-29
Quoddy, Me., 151, 153
Quoddy Head, 155

Redeemed Captive, The (Williams), 28
Rhode Island, 36-39
Ripton, Vt., 96
Roosevelt, Franklin Delano, 149, 153

Roosevelt, Theodore, 61
Round Pond, Me., 133-134
Roxbury, Conn., 8, 9, 10, 11, 12, 13
Russell, William, 56

St. Croix Island (Me.), 151
St. David, Me., 168, 170-171
Saint-Gaudens, Augustus, 80-82, 84
St. George, Me., 141
St. John River Valley, 158, 169-175
St. Johnsbury, Vt., 122
St. Regis River, 158
Samoset (Indian leader), 133
Sanctuary (MacKaye), 84
Sanderson Brook Falls, 35
Sandwich, N.H., 90, 91-94
Sandwich Home Industries, 93
Scott Bridge, 62
Scourge of the Aristocracy, The (Lyon), 16
Sebec Lake, 162
Second Lake, 125
Sedgwick, Catharine, 31
Shakers, 20-21, 66, 86-87, 110
Shannock, R.I., 39
Sharon, Conn., 8, 14, 18-19
Shays' Rebellion, 24-25
Sheepscot, Me., 135
Sheepscot River, 135
Sheffield, Vt., 121
Shepaug River, 8
Shirley Mills, Me., 162
Sky Lodge, 162
Smith, Aza, 75
Smith, Captain John, 131, 138
Smith (Helen Woodruff) Sanctuary, 84
Smyrna Mills, Me., 165
South Britain, Conn., 8, 12, 13
South Cornish, Vt., 82-83
Southfield, Mass., 21
South Stoddard, N.H., 52
South Sutton, N.H., 64
South Wheelock, Vt., 121
Springfield, Mass., 25
Spruce Head, Me., 141
Squam Lake, 93
Stark, N.H., 116-117
Sterling Institute, 108-109, 113
Stewartstown Hollow, N.H., 124, 125
Stockholm, Me., 173, 174
Stoddard, N.H., 52-53
Strolls by Starlight and Sunshine (Gibson), 11
Stuart, Gilbert, 38, 39
Sugarloaf, Mount, 24, 25, 26-27
Sugar River, 70, 71

Sutton, N.H., 64
Sutton, Vt., 121
Swansea, Mass., 36
Sweden, Me., 173

Tecumseh Mountain, 91
Temple, N.H., 53
Tenants Harbor, Me., 141, 142
"Thanatopsis" (Bryant), 30-31, 35
Thayer, Abbott, 50
13 Mile Woods, 127
Thomas, William Widgery, Jr., 174
Thoreau, Henry David, 49, 61
Tobacco Valley, 24
Tolstoi, Count Ilya, 13
Townshend, Vt., 62
Tripyramid Mountain, 91
Turners Falls, Mass., 29
Twain, Mark, 22, 50
Tyringham, Mass., 20-23

Umbagog Lake, 125
United Society of Believers, see Shakers

Van Buren, Me., 171, 172
Vermont, 54-63, 74-84, 95-113, 117-121, 122
Vermont Historical Society Museum, 98, 103, 105
Victory, Vt., 120
Victory Bog, 121

Wabanaki Confederacy, 151
Wadleigh State Park, N.H., 64
Waitsfield, Vt., 97
Waldo, General Samuel, 130
Waldoboro, Me., 130-131, 175
Walpole, Vt., 57
Wampanoag Indians, 36
Wamsutta (Indian leader), 36
Warner, Seth, 10, 11
Warren, Vt., 99, 100-101

Washington, Conn., 8, 9, 10-11, 13, 68, 69
Washington, Mount, 49
Washington, N.H., 64, 65-66, 69
Webster, Daniel, 127, 170
Webster Lake, 85
Wells, Vt., 95
Wentworth, Benning, 57, 70
Wesley, Me., 143, 148
West Chesterfield, Mass., 35
West Claremont, N.H., 73
West Cornwall, Conn., 14-15, 16
Westfield, Vt., 112
West Forks, Me., 158, 162
Westport, Conn., 119
West Townshend, Vt., 62
Weymouth, Captain George, 138
Whateley, Mass., 24, 28, 29
Whiteface Mountain, 91
Whitefield, Me., 135
White Mountain National Forest, 115
White Mountains, 91-94, 127
Whitneyville, Me., 143
Williams, Reverend John, 28
Williams, Roger, 36
Willoughby, Lake, 121
Wilson, Woodrow, 61, 80, 84
Windham Foundation, 61
Windsor, Vt., 80, 83
Winnipesaukee, Lake, 94
Winslow, Me., 119
Winooski River Valley, 98, 104
"Winter Sunrise, Monadnock" (Thayer), 50
Wood, William, 45
Woodbury, Conn., 8-10, 11, 13
Woodbury, Vt., 102, 104
Woodstock, N.H., 66
Worcester, Vt., 104
Worden Pond, 39
Wright, Reverend Chester, 66-67
Wykeham Rise, 11
Wyman Dam, 158

Yankee magazine, 50